A SLOW RIDE INTO THE PAST

A SLOW RIDE INTO THE PAST

THE CHINESE TRISHAW INDUSTRY IN SINGAPORE, 1942–1983

JASON LIM

© Copyright 2013 Jason Lim
All rights reserved. Apart from any uses permitted by Australia's Copyright Act 1968, no part of this book may be reproduced by any process without prior written permission from the copyright owners. Inquiries should be directed to the publisher.

Monash University Publishing
Building 4, Monash University
Clayton, Victoria 3800, Australia
www.publishing.monash.edu
www.publishing.monash.edu/books/srp-9781921867385.html

Monash University Publishing brings to the world publications which advance the best traditions of humane and enlightened thought. Monash University Publishing titles pass through a rigorous process of independent peer review.

Design: Les Thomas
Cover images: front cover – a trishaw rider and a rickshaw puller on Bras Basah Road 15 April 1941 – courtesy of the National Archives of Singapore; back cover – trishaws lined up before the charity ride for the National Defence Fund in 1968 – courtesy of the National Archives of Singapore.

This book is part of the **Monash Asia Series**. The Monash Asia Series comprises works that make a significant contribution to our understanding of one or more Asian nations or regions. The individual works that make up this multi-disciplinary series are selected on the basis of their contemporary relevance. The Monash Asia Series of the Monash Asia Institute replaces Monash University's MAI Press imprint, which, from the early 1970s, has demonstrated this University's strong interest and expertise in Asian studies.

Monash Asia Series Editorial Board
Professor Marika Vicziany, Chair, Professor of Asian Political Economy, Monash Asia Institute, Faculty of Arts
Professor Greg Barton, School of Political and Social Inquiry, Faculty of Arts
Assoc. Professor Gloria Davies, School of Languages, Cultures and Linguistics, Faculty of Arts
Dr Julian Millie, School of Political and Social Inquiry, Faculty of Arts
Dr Jagjit Plahe, Department of Management, Faculty of Business and Economics
Dr David Templeman, School of Philosophical, Historical and International Studies, Faculty of Arts

National Library of Australia Cataloguing-in-Publication entry
Author: Lim, Jason, 1971-
Title: A slow ride into the past: the Chinese trishaw industry in Singapore, 1942-1983/Jason Lim.
ISBN: 9781921867385 (pbk.)
Subjects: Pedicabs--Singapore--History; Pedicab drivers--Singapore--History.
Dewey Number: 388.41320959

Printed in Australia by Griffin Press an Accredited ISO AS/NZS 14001:2004 Environmental Management System printer.

The paper this book is printed on is certified by the Programme for the Endorsement of Forest Certification scheme. Griffin Press holds PEFC chain of custody SGS - PEFC/COC-0594. PEFC promotes environmentally responsible, socially beneficial and economically viable management of the world's forests.

FOREWORD

Dr Lim's study of the trishaw industry in Singapore between 1942 and 1983 represents a significant and welcome contribution to the social and labour history of Singapore. His study makes a strong case for attention to be paid to those individuals whose lives are often swept under the carpet of history and builds on some fine work that has already been done by other historians with an interest in Singapore over the past several decades. It complements and builds superbly on the history of rickshaws in Singapore undertaken for an earlier period by James Warren. Anyone concerned with more nuanced historical studies will applaud the extent to which this history takes the reader on a journey that links traditional historical practice (archival) with new methods approaches (oral history and photography). In doing so the reader explores not only the lives of one occupational group but also the interconnected nature of elite and non-elite stories in the fabric of Singapore's modern history. The study also demonstrates the connectedness of ordinary individuals' lives in broader global historical movements and change. Lim's work is wonderful evidence of the vibrancy of social history and of a younger generation of Singaporean historians who want a more inclusive Singapore story.

– *Associate Professor Stephen Dobbs*
Chair, Asian Studies
The University of Western Australia

CONTENTS

Foreword v

Acknowledgements ix

Abbreviations xi

Map 1: Fujian province, 1820. xiii

Map 2: Singapore city area, 1947 xiv

Introduction: Social history of the Chinese community in Singapore xv

Chapter 1: Cycle transport in Southeast Asia 1

Chapter 2: The advent of the trishaws 14

Chapter 3: The trishaw industry as a '*bang*'-based trade 38

Chapter 4: The trishaw industry and Singapore society 79

Chapter 5: The twilight years 108

Conclusion: The trishaw industry in perspective 123

Appendix 1 127

Appendix 2 129

Appendix 3 130

Appendix 4 132

Appendix 5 133

Appendix 6 134

Appendix 7 135

Appendix 8 136

Appendix 9 137

Appendix 10 138

APPENDIX 11	141
APPENDIX 12	143
APPENDIX 13	144
APPENDIX 14	146
BIBLIOGRAPHY	147
INDEX	161

ACKNOWLEDGEMENTS

This publication is based on my Honours thesis '"Sor Leng Ngia": The Rise and Demise of the Trishaw Industry in Singapore, 1945–1983', which was submitted to Murdoch University in 1995. Over the course of my research work the trishaw industry virtually died, although a few elderly riders could still be seen plying the streets. In 1999 I thought of reworking the thesis for publication. Unfortunately, due to pressures from work, I had neither the time nor the energy to edit and update the original manuscript.

It was only after I had finished my PhD dissertation at the University of Western Australia that I could – for about a year at least – find the time to rework my old Honours thesis. By then, 12 years had passed and the old trishaw industry was no more. This book, then, is a tribute to those trishaw riders who had faithfully plied the streets of Singapore from World War II to the end of the twentieth century. With trishaw riding still fresh in the minds of people in Singapore, this is certainly a fitting time to finally publish the manuscript! I owe a debt of gratitude and love to my wife Bee Leng, my parents, my brother and his family for their tremendous support and encouragement as I restarted work on the trishaw industry.

The person to whom I wish to record my greatest thanks, for his encouragement and feedback, is my Honours supervisor, Professor James Francis Warren. Back in 1995 he had been patient with me and had provided valuable guidance in preparing the original manuscript. Even after my graduation from Murdoch University, we continued to correspond on some new directions and ideas for the manuscript.

A number of institutions deserve special thanks for giving me access to key documents and secondary sources. These include the Libraries of the National University of Singapore; Resource Centre of the Singapore Federation of Chinese Clan Associations; Murdoch University Library; National Archives of Singapore (NAS); Information Resource Centre of Singapore Press Holdings (SPH); Lee Kong Chian Reference Library, National Library Board; Hin Ann Huay Kuan; Singapore Futsing Association (SFA); Registry of Vehicles; Registry of Societies; Registry of Mutual Benefit Organisations; Reid Library, The University of Western Australia; Library of Monash University; Registry of Trade Unions and the Ministry of Community Development, Youth and Sports. I must acknowledge the contributions given by Madam Ong Chwee Lan, daughter of a former trishaw owner whom I interviewed in 1995, and the late Mr Chan Kwee Sung, who handed me some personal notes when I met him that same year. The Imperial War Museum in London, the National Archives & Records Administration at College Park in Maryland, the Ministry of Information, Communications and the Arts in Singapore, Mr Lim Kheng Chye, Mr Paul Piollet, the SPH and the NAS also gave me permission to use their photographs.

I want to thank the then Monash Asia Institute Press (now the Monash Asia Series of Monash University Publishing) and the Institute of Southeast Asian Studies, who thought that my manuscript was worth publishing, and the two anonymous reviewers for their very useful feedback. I also wish to thank Stephen Dobbs for writing the Foreword. My appreciation is similarly extended to the Malaysian Branch of the Royal Asiatic Society, which gave its permission to use the article 'The Trishaw Industry as a "Bang"-based Trade' as Chapter Three of this book. It was originally published in Volume 69, Part 2, of the *Journal of the Malaysian Branch of the Royal Asiatic Society* in December 1996.

This publication is made possible by a Publication Subsidy from the Chiang Ching-Kuo Foundation for International Scholarly Exchange in Taipei.

ABBREVIATIONS

AGM	Annual General Meeting
ARMCS	Administration Report of the Municipal Council of Singapore
ARROV	Annual Report of the Registry of Vehicles
ARSS	Annual Report of the Straits Settlements
ARVRD	Annual Report of the Vehicles Registration Department
BMA	British Military Administration
CID	Criminal Investigation Department
CSGGS	Colony of Singapore Government Gazette Supplement
GLU	General Labour Union
HDB	Housing & Development Board
LF	Labour Front
MMC	Minutes of the Municipal Council
MPCCS	Minutes of the Proceedings of the City Council of Singapore
MPMCS	Minutes of the Proceedings of the Municipal Commission, Singapore
MRT	Mass Rapid Transit
MUI	Malaysian United Industries
NAS	National Archives of Singapore
NDF	National Defence Fund (1968)
OHC	Oral History Centre (a division of the NAS)
PAP	People's Action Party
RMBO	Registry of Mutual Benefit Organisations
ROS	Registry of Societies
ROV	Registry of Vehicles
RTD	Road Transport Department
RTU	Registry of Trade Unions
SBS	Singapore Bus Service
SCCC	Singapore Chinese Chamber of Commerce
SFA	Singapore Futsing Association
SFTU	Singapore Federation of Trade Unions
SHTRA	Singapore Hired Trishaw Riders Association

SHTRMBO	Singapore Hired Trishaw Riders Mutual Benefit Organisation
SIT	Singapore Improvement Trust
SMAR	Singapore Municipality Annual Report
SPH	Singapore Press Holdings
SRTWU	Singapore Rickshaw and Trishaw Workers Union
SSAR	Straits Settlements Annual Report
STC	Singapore Traction Company
STOA	Singapore Trishaw Owners Association
STPB	Singapore Tourist Promotion Board
SYB	Singapore Year Book
SWD	Social Welfare Department
TIPMAS	Trishaw Industry Proprietors and Manufacturers Association of Singapore
VRD	Vehicles Registration Department

MAP 1: FUJIAN PROVINCE, 1820

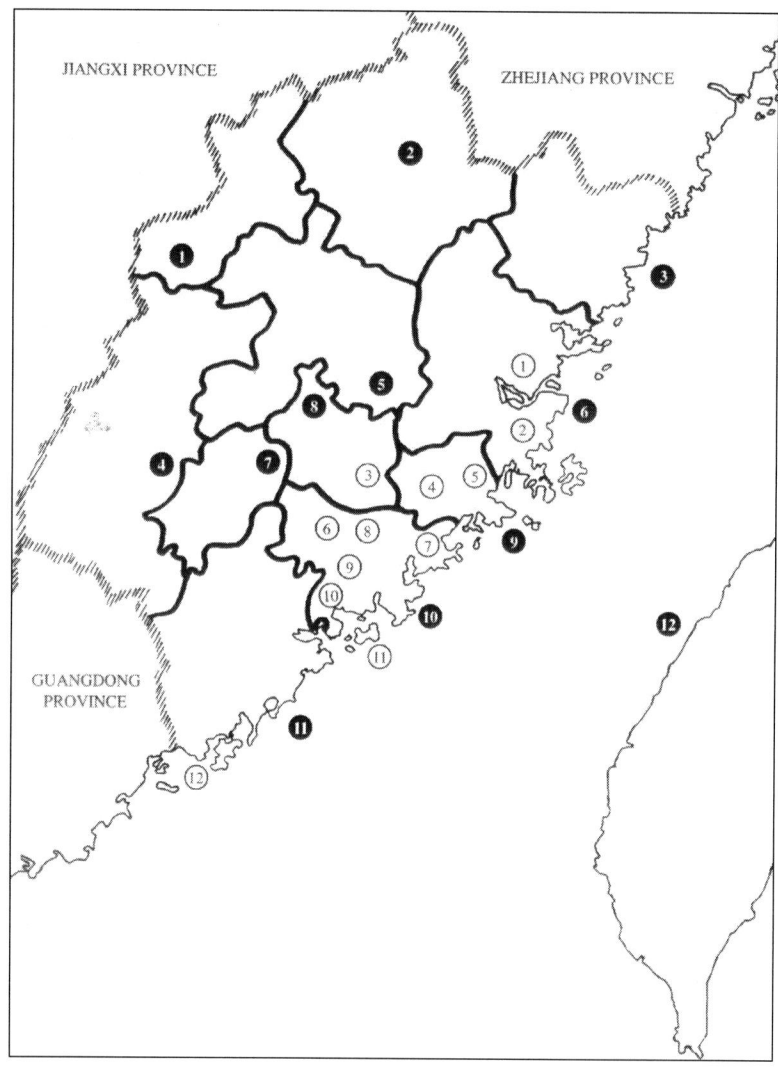

The Chinese had begun migrating from the province to Singapore after a trading post was established on the island the year before. Fujian was further sub-divided into 12 prefectures (numbered in black circles):

(1) Shaowu
(2) Jianning
(3) Funing
(4) Tingzhou
(5) Yanping
(6) Fuzhou
(7) Longyan
(8) Yongchun
(9) Xinghua
(10) Quanzhou
(11) Zhangzhou
(12) Taiwan

Migrants also departed from the following major districts and cities (numbered in white circles):

(1) Fuzhou
(2) Fuqing
(3) Yongchun
(4) Xianyou
(5) Putian
(6) Anxi
(7) Huian
(8) Nan'an
(9) Jinjiang
(10) Xiamen
(11) Jinmen
(12) Zhaoan.

The Henghuas came from Xinghua Prefecture, the Hokchias from Xianyou and Putian districts and the Hui Ann Hokkiens from Huian District.

MAP 2: SINGAPORE CITY AREA, 1947

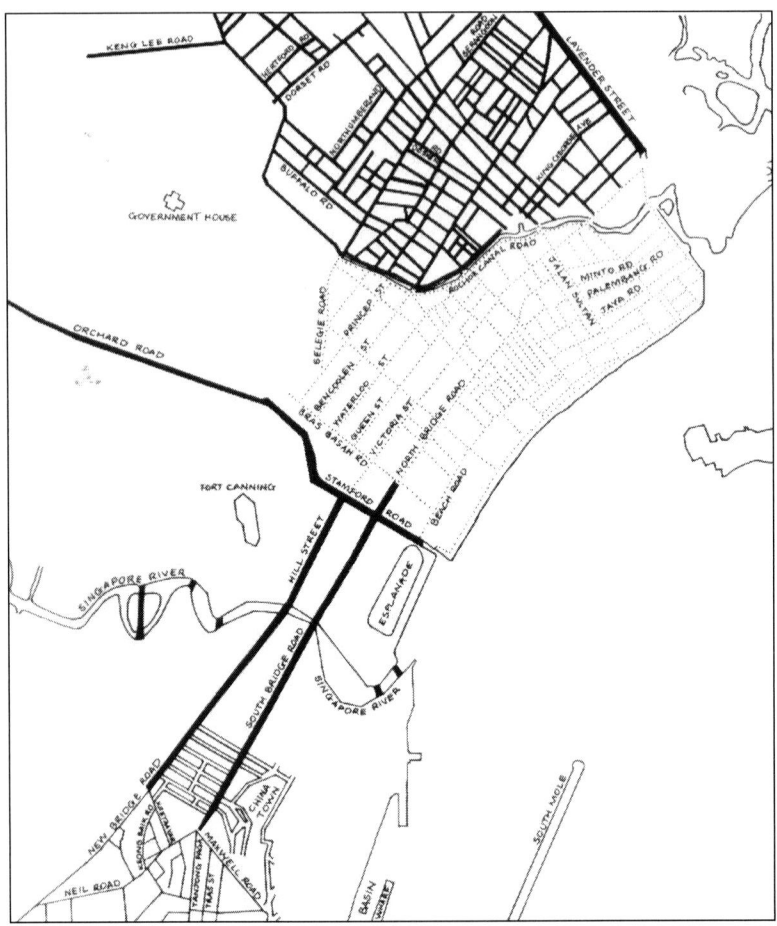

The city area of Singapore in 1947, showing the location of Chinatown (bottom), postal District 7 (roads in dotted lines) and postal District 8 (top, roads in dark lines).

Introduction

SOCIAL HISTORY OF THE CHINESE COMMUNITY IN SINGAPORE

Social historians today are expanding the analytical and methodological boundaries of history by exploring the everyday lives of people from the lower echelons of society. Attention has shifted to ordinary people who have played a significant developmental role in history, often through hard manual work, but whose societal contribution has often been overshadowed by that of the dominant elite. In the contemporary historiography of Singapore, one finds many written works on prominent merchants. These are important figures that, by virtue of their wealth, status and power, have shaped the political and economic development of modern Singapore. A common focus in the study of the overseas Chinese community in Singapore has been the life, business work and philanthropic contributions of prominent merchants in the belief that such a study would provide an inspiration for the next generation of Singaporeans to aspire to greater wealth and fame. Studies into the life of the merchants tend to concentrate on those prominent from the 1920s to the end of World War II such as Aw Boon Haw, Tan Lark Sye, Tan Kah Kee, Eu Tong Sen, Lee Kong Chian and Lim Chwee Chian (Chan & Chiang 1994; Chen 1967; Cheng 1987; Lin 1987; Lin 1990; Yang 1996; Yong 1987; Yong 1992; Zhong 2002).

Growing up in Singapore, it seems rather strange to the author that the history of the country should be so intricately bound up with such prominent figures. There were people who grew up in the 1950s who keep telling the next generation of Singaporeans (including the author) that 'life was tough' during that period. It becomes difficult to reconcile the fact that ordinary people could lead harsh lives and yet historical studies remain focussed on the rich and powerful. Indeed, the lives of the business elite have been studied to such an extent in Singapore that the historical record has been shut until recently on those who never moved upwards in terms of capital accumulation and social mobility.

This publication on the trishaw industry is in response to the general need for Singaporeans to be more aware of their national past. While it is a worthwhile exercise to look into the contributions of the merchants in the overseas Chinese community, one should not forget that the economic development of Singapore has been built on the backs of those who remained nowhere near the upper echelons of society. There is a need to 'invert the emphasis' (Warren 1986:3) and move towards a greater appreciation of the middle- and lower-classes in the community. To do this, we need to look beyond overused archival materials and secondary sources; we need to find novel ways of using other source materials, and to adopt new approaches towards historical research.

It is also the author's hope that, by 'enlarging the vision of history' (Zunz 1985:3), the social historian will be able to clarify and explain how ordinary people in a place like Singapore reacted towards local/global policies instituted by the nation-state as well as the advent of mass consumerism in an increasingly interconnected world. One methodological approach is through the careful use of oral history in order to give history and/or memory 'back to the people in their own words' (Thompson 1988:265). In this context, social history is also increasingly linked with cognisant disciplines which have not always been perceived as compatible with the overall aims and method of history – disciplines such as psychology, anthropology, human geography, sociology, statistics and linguistics. The standard historical format of chronological narration is supplemented by ideas and modes of social inquiry from these disciplines in order to re-interpret and re-present the history of society within a wider framework. One note of caution, however, is that the life, circumstance and contribution of lesser known ordinary individuals should be inextricably bound with the views and policies of the elite. The new social history and research methods are not to absolutely negate the contribution of the merchants and other elites.

The focus on magnates remained the fulcrum for historical research on the Chinese community in Singapore because of their leadership of the community, personal success or ethnicity. Edwin Lee noted that 'no one has done a full scale work on the social history of Singapore' although he comments favourably on CM Turnbull's several historical works, which are largely political in nature (Lee 1986:18). Nevertheless, arguably the initial attempt in Singapore at writing the new social history can be traced back to a project about the history of Singapore Chinese trades undertaken by

SOCIAL HISTORY OF THE CHINESE COMMUNITY

the History Department of Nanyang University between 1969 and 1971. The collection of oral history accounts was central to the project and one of the major reports, *The Henghuas and Land Transport*, is of some considerable significance for this publication (Nanyang Daxue Lishi Xi 1971).[1]

By the mid-1980s, changes in the historiography of the Singapore Chinese community emerged when Yen Ching-hwang and James Francis Warren published *A Social History of the Chinese in Singapore and Malaya* and *Rickshaw Coolie* respectively in 1986 (Warren 1986; Yen 1986). Here, the approaches by these two eminent historians differ in their study of a social history of Singapore. Yen looked at the social structure and functions of the Chinese community in Singapore and Malaya. He was keen to look at how the Chinese community organised themselves and how it dealt with social problems within the community. Yen inevitably highlighted the work of some merchants while looking at questions of community leadership and class structure. Numerous souvenir magazines and other publications from dialect and clan associations were used in his research but the problem with these publications is that they usually highlight prominent people within the associations. Unlike Yen, Warren took a totally different approach in his study of the rickshaw pullers. In his pioneering work, Warren used Coroner's records, oral history and government reports to recreate the life and circumstance of rickshaw pullers in colonial Singapore between 1880 and 1940. His innovative social history illustrated vividly how colonial policy *did not* benefit an urban occupational group – the rickshaw pullers – who experienced extreme suffering and a sense of vulnerability due to their low socio-economic status. Yet they provided a critically important means of public transport in the port city during those 60 years. Calling it 'the real stuff of urban social history', Warren wrote that 'it seems to me incredible to present a history of Singapore without the coolie' (Warren 1986:3–4). His research was based on the premise that people such as the ordinary rickshaw puller should be recognised for their contributions to the community and society at large.

Warren's work stemmed from his interest in uncovering the lives of those who lived in a 'culture of silence' by stepping outside the framework of history written by those with 'their own social bias' (*ARI News* 2004:1–2; Warren 1995). His research, therefore, places the coolies at the centre of Singapore's history. His work has been criticised but the negative comments

---

[1] Unfortunately, the report contains several historical inaccuracies and/or unsubstantiated views.

actually reveal the biases of the critics themselves. One reviewer complained that 'to argue that a people's history should be written because it had been hidden and neglected and because there happened to be records on such a wretched group in society is a weak reason for doing it'. He implied that there was no real need for such a study because it did not throw light on British administration and policy, the rural-urban divide or Chinese immigration (Lian 1992:99). This view would leave a very narrow scope for historical research into the Chinese community. Yen himself also referred to *Rickshaw Coolie* as the history of only one segment of overseas Chinese society in Singapore. Yen insisted that the history of the rickshaw pullers should not be taken as the basis for the history of the entire community (not that this was ever Warren's assertion anyway) as their lives could not be used as a representation of the organisation and development of Chinese society in Singapore (Yan 2005:263). However, these remarks in a similar vein can be applied as a criticism of current studies on the Chinese in Singapore. If the lives of rickshaw pullers should be rejected as representative of Chinese society, why then must the history of the magnates be taken as the basis for understanding the history of the entire community? Should the lives of the rich be accepted while those of the rest forgotten? This raises questions about accepting the lives of magnates as historical evidence while marginalising the lives of everyone else in historical research.

In 2003 another work about the lives of coolies was published: *The Singapore River*, by Stephen Dobbs. In this instance, the work is about hardship as a coolie working on the banks of the Singapore River (Dobbs 2003). This publication on the trishaw industry is built on that same premise. The trishaw industry was chosen because of the challenges it had to face – from the authorities and the public at large – as Singapore progressed from Crown Colony to self-governing State to an independent Republic. The trishaws were ubiquitous in the late 1940s and early 1950s. As time progressed, a combination of government policies and negative public perceptions caused the industry to be increasingly sidelined, with the result that it was seen as an obsolete form of public transport by the 1980s.

Sources and approach

If Warren found it difficult to accept a history of Singapore without the coolie, I have found it strange that, to-date, no historical study has been done on the Chinese trishaw industry in Singapore, even though trishaws provided a key mode of public transport from the 1940s to the 1980s. Two contemporaneous works exist: a study of the lives of 40 trishaw riders by Wee Soo Hup (1962) and the project on *The Henghuas and Land Transport* by the History Department of Nanyang University mentioned earlier (Nanyang Daxue Lishi Xi 1971). Wee had difficulty preparing his thesis in 1962 – he found that although the Research Section of the Social Welfare Department had carried out a survey of trishaw riders in 1955, the report was somehow not publicly available (Wee 1962:1–2).

Since this book is about the rise and decline of trishaws as a means of public transport in Singapore and the lives of those who plied in the trade, I have to look at other government sources such as official records from the Municipal Commission (replaced by the City Council in 1951), the State Government and various government departments. I also need access to unpublished records from trishaw owners' and riders' associations, oral history recordings, photographs and personal memoirs. As regulators of the trishaw industry, one cannot ignore the records of the Municipal Commission and City Council as well as the records of the Registry of Societies, Registry of Trade Unions, and the Labour Department as these government departments had to deal with problems posed by the trishaw owners and/or riders.

The unpublished minutes of meetings and correspondence of the Singapore Trishaw Owners Association (STOA) and the Singapore Hired Trishaw Riders Association (SHTRA) reveal the challenges faced by the trishaw industry from the 1950s to the 1970s. Unfortunately, the records of the SHTRA held at the NAS stop at 1976, the year the NAS stopped acquiring records from the association. It means that a look at the critical period from 1976 to 1983 (when the SHTRA was finally dissolved) had to be done through old newspaper clippings and oral history recordings. The Oral History Centre (OHC) at NAS had also conducted interviews with several trishaw riders as part of its 'Chinese Dialect Groups' project begun in 1986. These riders spoke candidly about their personal backgrounds, migration to Singapore and how they switched from rickshaw pulling to trishaw riding. Almost 19 hours of interviews were recorded (Lim 2005:167–189). The recordings are a boon to this publication because the trishaw riders constitute just one occupational group 'who had previously been considered too unimportant to merit much attention since *they were too ordinary*' (Caunce 1994:7–8).

The period from the 1950s to the 1970s was also one where European travellers visited Singapore and penned their memoirs on their return home. Several of them took a ride in a trishaw in Singapore and decided that it was worth writing about this experience in their travelogues. Added to their memories of the trishaw industry is the presence of old photographs of street scenes in the city area, many of which show the heavy presence of trishaws, particularly in the 1950s. It adds credence to the belief that the humble trishaw was a crucial and popular mode of public transport in the 1950s, until the bus and taxi companies began improving their fleet of vehicles and the trishaw came to be considered a relic of the past.

Katherine Yeo has perceptively argued that 'the uniqueness and the nature … of the life of coolies in different "segments" of society inevitably calls for further research' (Yeo 1989:1). She has written a fine thesis on Singapore hawkers – one 'segment' of coolie society – under colonial rule from the mid-nineteenth century to 1939. The research I present here is in a similar vein, seeking to describe and analyse how changes in the state and society affected another particular 'segment' of contemporary Singapore society. In this case, it is a history about those people involved in the trishaw industry – the owners and the riders – from 1942 to 1983. The period starts in 1942 when the Japanese Occupation of Singapore commenced and trishaws first appeared on the city streets. Rickshaws were still present but the trishaw industry flourished with the ban on rickshaws in 1947. This history closes in 1983, the year that saw the final demise of the industry with the dissolution of the trishaw riders' association.

Outline of the book

The purpose of this book is to locate the history of the trishaw industry within the wider framework of political and social changes in Singapore and the transformation of her human landscape since 1942. The next chapter looks at the situation faced by trishaw riders across Southeast Asia in order to make a comparison between their experiences and those of the Chinese trishaw riders in Singapore. Chapter Two introduces the advent of the trishaws. It also analyses the effects of the ban on rickshaws in 1947 as well as the design, manufacture and repair of trishaws. Chapter Three examines the trishaw industry within the socio-economic concept of a *bang*-based Singapore Chinese society. The origin of the Henghuas and Hokchias, the two main dialect groups involved in the industry, is noted. This is followed by a discussion of the role of the three key trishaw-based organisations. Chapter Four focusses on the roles of the trishaw industry within general

Singapore society and how the public, local and state government, and foreigners perceived the vehicles and riders.

The two final chapters study how and why the industry declined. As time passed, the Singapore urban landscape and transport system began to change dramatically. Changes also occurred in the public's view of what constituted an acceptable form of work and a decent wage. The trishaw industry, therefore, had to deal with changes in public thinking and attitudes as well by the early 1970s. The book ends with an investigation of how the trishaw-based organisations reacted to the modern development of Singapore during those 41 years.

Chapter 1

CYCLE TRANSPORT IN SOUTHEAST ASIA

Introduction

The trishaw was a popular means of transport in Singapore from the end of World War II until its slow decline in the 1970s. This mode of cycle transport was by no means a ubiquitous scene only in Singapore; it was also a popular form of low-cost public transport across Southeast Asia. Introduced in the region in different time periods, the trishaw consists of a carriage with the seat usually set very low with a canopy over the head to protect the passenger(s) against rain and attached to the frame of a bicycle. Trishaws were found throughout Southeast Asia but they all looked different from one another. In Singapore, Malacca, Vientiane and Kota Bahru, the carriage was on the left side of the bicycle. In Penang, Jakarta, Yogyakarta, Ujung Pandang, Phnom Penh, Hanoi and Ho Chi Minh City, the carriage was situated in front of the trishaw rider. The trishaws in parts of Thailand was unique in this respect with the rider pedalling in front of the carriage.

There are detailed studies focussing on the structure of the trishaw industry and the plight of trishaw riders in Bangkok, Singapore, Penang, Kota Bahru, Malacca, Yogyakarta, Ujung Pandang and Jakarta. However, many of these studies were not conducted on the trishaw industry per se but rather on the industry as an integral part of the 'informal' sector and/or urban environment. For example, Forbes' work on trishaw riders in Ujung Pandang was conducted as part of an overall analysis of the 'informal' sector – characterised by 'its relative ease of entry for new enterprises, heavy reliance on indigenous resources, family ownership, small-scale operation, unregulated and competitive markets, labour-intensive and adapted technology, and skills acquired outside the formal education system' (Forbes 1979) – that thrived in South Sulawesi. Rimmer, on the other hand, focussed on the fate of trishaws in Southeast Asian cities faced with increasing urbanisation (Rimmer 1986:107–230).

Another notable emphasis in these accounts is the focus on the evolution of the industry itself across time. Sources published in the 1950s and 1960s such as Textor's report on northeastern farmers who migrated to Bangkok still concentrated on the relative strength of the trishaw industry, even though the Thai government had moved to limit the number of trishaws in Bangkok. The trishaws were introduced by the Thais in 1933 and as an occupation, pedalling them was 'restricted' to Thais only (Textor 1961:2). Textor did a detailed study of Thai trishaw riders: their attitudes towards the police; kinship and friendship; income and expenditure; food, health and religion (Textor 1961:19–46). By the late 1970s, surveys of the trishaw industries in Southeast Asia painted a very bleak future. By this time, governments in the region had already voiced their desire to force trishaws off the streets through various measures such as not issuing new licenses (Penang in 1975), prohibiting trishaws from entering the city centre during certain hours (Jakarta in 1971 and Singapore in 1974) and introducing new motorised transport especially mini-buses or motorised trishaws to replace pedal trishaws (Surabaya in 1962 and Chiang Mai in 1971). Trishaws were seen by governments in Southeast Asia as a 'separate, unidentifiable network outside [the] national interests in transportation' (Beenhakker 1989:629). Several researchers, however, had argued for the retention of trishaws since they served the travelling needs of a substantial portion of the local population (Replogle 1989:654; Kartodirdjo 1981:118; Forbes 1978:1; Forbes 1979:165; Socio-Economic Research and Central Planning Unit 1979:27–28; Rimmer 1982b:64). Furthermore, researchers argued that banning trishaws would be a form of economic suicide since it would deprive many riders of employment. As these ex-trishaw riders would be unlikely to switch to providing motorised public transport, unemployment would soar. For instance, there were 17,000 trishaw riders in Ujung Pandang in 1975, about 15 per cent of the total population (Forbes 1978:220). Rimmer also noted that in Indonesia, few trishaw riders became taxi riders in the end (Rimmer 1982b:65). The real issue at stake for the various authorities was to ban trishaws because they projected an image of underdevelopment (Rimmer 1978:205). Yet, during an economic crisis in 1998, trishaws made a surprising comeback in the streets of Jakarta (Dick 2005:86).

Trishaws in Southeast Asia were also frequently mentioned in travel guides and travellers' accounts. Written primarily with the purpose of introducing various Southeast Asian cities to first-time travellers, these books often gave a romanticised or picturesque image of trishaws in the city. Indeed, 'tourists form an important source of pedal trishaws' revenue ... where they appear to represent part of the "Asian experience"' (Spencer 1989:203). These travel guides glossed over the hard life of trishaw riders and the frequent attempts to ban trishaws in various Southeast Asian cities. There were also books written by travellers about their stay – regardless of duration – in particular Southeast Asian cities. Here, trishaws were normally mentioned in passing although some gave detailed descriptions and personal opinions and anecdotes about the trishaws and their place in the urban landscape. For instance, the strength and ability required to cycle resulted in frequent anatomical references to the legs of trishaw riders. James Kirkup, travelling in Phnom Penh in the 1960s, thought of putting a small hand mirror through the rear window of the canvas hood so that one could observe the 'superb action of the driver's thighs' (Kirkup 1969:134). Swinstead and Haddon, writing about trishaw riders of Singapore in 1981, told readers they should take a ride from 'the often frail-looking but nevertheless wiry elder moving on wheels'. Readers were told not to feel sorry for the riders because 'their legs have given them all the wealth they require' (Swinstead & Haddon 1981:20). The authors conveniently ignored the fact that trishaw riding was hard work.

The lives of trishaw riders in Southeast Asia

Trishaw riders occupied a low status in society. In Yogyakarta, this status and the public perception of their trade resulted in 'a feeling in certain regions' that people could humiliate the trishaw rider by 'exploiting his manpower' (Kartodirdjo 1981:3). Many of these Javanese trishaw riders were migrant labourers. They entered the city to become trishaw riders because of the extreme poverty in the rural regions of Java where they had originated from. They were attracted to the trishaw industry by the relative ease of finding work as a rider. However, when it was harvest time in the countryside, these trishaw riders returned home, only to return to the city when harvesting was over. In a sample of 250 trishaw riders, about 55 per cent came from families who worked as farmers. Interestingly, it appeared that more farmers' sons became trishaw riders as compared to sons of trishaw riders. Obviously, with increasing loss of land in the countryside, trishaw riding had become one way to supplement family income (Kartodirdjo 1981:52). In Bangkok in the 1950s, many riders migrated from the northeastern provinces of Thailand and settled in Bangkok due to the harsh economic conditions in their home villages (Textor 1961:15). Out of nearly 5,000 riders who applied for validation of licenses in Bangkok in 1953, almost 66 per cent came from seven provinces in the northeast (Textor 1961:7–9). In Ujung Pandang, 87 per cent of all trishaw riders interviewed by Forbes between 1975 and 1976 were born in rural South Sulawesi (Forbes 1978:223). In Penang and Singapore, however, the trishaw riders were from the islands themselves. In a survey of Penang riders in 1979, it was found that nearly 70 per cent of them were from Penang Island itself, with another 20 per cent from other Malaysian states (Socio-Economic Research and Central Planning Unit 1979:6). In Singapore, it had long been recognised among the Chinese population that trishaw riding was the work of men from the minority Henghua and Hokchia dialect groups. Many of them were former rickshaw pullers who had migrated from China before the war and switched to trishaw riding upon the abolition of rickshaws in 1947 (Nanyang Daxue Lishi Xi 1971).

Despite being on the bottom end of the occupation scale in society, the trishaw riders provided a critical means of transport prior to the advent of mass rapid motorised transport. Their procedures for seeking passengers were similar throughout Southeast Asia. Generally, there were two groups of trishaw riders: a group that cruised around the streets looking for potential passengers and another group that chose to wait patiently in a trishaw park. In the latter case, a passenger could choose who he/she would want to hire, the fare was bargained before the trip (unless the fares were gazetted) and the trishaw rider would then cycle off with the passenger. In Ujung Pandang, for instance, many trishaws in the city would congregate at particular points known as *stanplat*. Some *stanplat* were huge, with several hundred trishaws waiting for custom. There also appeared to be ethnically based stands as Forbes found that the largest at Pasar Sentral was a *stanplat* solely for Bugis trishaw riders (Forbes 1979:166). In Bangkok prior to the ban in 1960, there appeared to be so-called 'parking gangs' who would ensure that no conflict would occur between the trishaw riders from different regions over competition for potential passengers. These trishaw parks were officially designated by the police and most of the better parks were monopolised by non-Northeastern riders (Textor 1961:22–23). Rimmer's survey of 112 Georgetown trishaw riders in Penang revealed that those who chose to wait for passengers at stands were usually better educated, had a better command of English and were younger. They became trishaw riders upon leaving a previous job and thus rode for fewer years than those who had been cruising the streets. The latter usually took up trishaw riding because there was 'no other work' for them (Rimmer 1982a:151–152).

The way trishaw riders rented vehicles from owners was also similar across Southeast Asia. A new rider would be introduced to a trishaw owner through an acquaintance or a relative, who must be someone known and trusted by the owner. In Bangkok, after paying a 100 baht deposit, the rental fee was then determined according to the condition of the trishaw. In a tacit policy of discrimination, trishaw riders from Bangkok were charged lower rents than those from northeast Thailand. Older northeasterners were charged lower rates than the newly arrived (Textor 1961:28). In Yogyakarta, only 12.8 per cent of trishaw riders owned their own vehicles. The common practice for remaining riders was to produce a citizen identification card in order to rent a trishaw from the owner. A guarantee from a friend was also required to prevent the trishaw rider from avoiding the rental fee (Kartodirdjo 1981:38–40).

The main expenses after paying the rental fee were for food and clothing, and accommodation if they lived in a rented room or flat. In Penang in 1979, an estimated 76 per cent of trishaw riders surveyed spent M$110 on food per month out of an average wage of between M$101 and M$200 per month. Interestingly, while 62 per cent of trishaw riders spent a maximum of M$40 on clothes, another 31 per cent never bought new apparel. Instead, they used second-hand clothing donated by individuals (Socio-Economic Research and Central Planning Unit 1979:10). In Bangkok, where the average daily income was between 30 to 50 baht per day in the 1950s, many trishaw riders spent about 15 baht a day on food, drinks and tobacco. Clothes did not matter much: however, some spent as much as 50 baht per month on apparel while others always wore their uniforms (Textor 1961:29).

Accommodation for trishaw riders was cheap but the living conditions were generally poor. In Ujung Pandang, about half of 111 trishaw riders interviewed owned their own homes in 1979 and another 36 per cent lived in rented or contracted lodgings. Although home ownership among trishaw riders was high, with rents averaging 500 to 1,000 rupiah per month, the living conditions of most premises were lamentable. Consequently, many trishaw riders spent considerable amounts of money renovating their homes (Forbes 1979:237–238). Some trishaw riders stayed at places that required little or no rent at all. In Bangkok, for instance, many trishaw riders lived in places owned by trishaw owners, which meant that lodging was either free or at most one baht a day. Other riders communally shared the cost of a rented house, or stayed with relatives for fee, or even lodged in Buddhist temples (Textor 1961:29). In Yogyakarta, in a sample of 250 trishaw riders, about 48 per cent still went back home to their villages while 16 per cent owned their own homes within the city itself. Of those who did not own their own homes, about 32 per cent lived in rented accommodation paid for on a monthly basis. Among the least fortunate, there were some trishaw riders who slept in their own vehicles in bus terminals, railway stations and 'in no certain place' (Kartodirdjo 1981:59–60). In Singapore, trishaw riders 'never led good lives'. At best, they lived in government-built one-room flats with their *entire family*. The rest lived in attap or zinc-roofed houses, old shophouses, along corridors or within the trishaws (Nanyang Daxue Lishi Xi 1971:61).

A final socio-economic barometer of the status of trishaw riders in Southeast Asia was their education level. The huge majority of trishaw riders never advanced beyond primary school, which partly explained their decision to become trishaw riders (Socio-Economic Research and Central Planning Unit 1979:6; Bariman 1983:4; Kartodirdjo 1981:50). In Yogyakarta, about 39 per cent of the sample of 250 trishaw riders never completed primary school, with another 23 per cent only finishing their primary education (Kartodirdjo 1981:50). As one man recalled, 'some people I know ... became trishaw drivers out of desperation' since they had only a primary education (Smithies 1982:56). The situation in East Java, on the other hand, was worse: in a sample of 386 trishaw riders, about 36 per cent did not complete elementary school and an additional 33 per cent never went to school at all (Bariman 1983:6). In Penang, almost three-quarters of a sample of 154 trishaw riders had a primary education with half of them never completing it. This survey also noted that the majority of those who never went to school or completed a primary education were older trishaw riders of about the age of 41. Younger trishaw riders had a better education. With such a low general level of education, in times of economic hardship in both Yogyakarta and Penang, trishaw riding was one of the few rational choices open to unskilled individuals.

It is safe to conclude that the riders all shared certain common characteristics: they had a low educational level; incomes were rarely fixed due to the fluctuating number of fares; a significant portion of their income was spent on renting the trishaw (if they were not owner-pedallers), on food and on dependents (if any); their accommodation was poor; and they occupied the lower echelons of society. In Singapore, their status was so low one source noted sarcastically that 'their presence would put those who talked about the goodness of humanity to shame' (Nanyang Daxue Lishi Xi 1971:61).

One observation that stood out in the major studies conducted on the trishaw riders across Southeast Asia in different time periods was that, as a result of the social stigma of being situated at the lower end of society, many riders became disillusioned with their jobs. Some actually left the trade of their own accord. The men who migrated from the countryside to Ujung Pandang to become trishaw riders were increasingly disenchanted with their lives since it meant separation from their families and villages. Moreover, they grew disillusioned with urban life in the city itself (Forbes 1978:231).

In Bangkok, the trishaw riders grew wary from constant discrimination and exploitation by fellow riders who were Bangkok residents. There were three metropolitan trishaw riders' unions but these unions were shut out to trishaw riders who were neither Bangkok nor Thonburi residents. Textor concluded that:

> Suffice to say, with all candor, that in many hypothetical cases it is probably just as well, in the short run, that there have not been associations devoted to enhancing the welfare of the Northeastern pedicab drivers in Bangkok. Such associations would too likely have led to exploitation rather than benevolence (Textor 1961:27).

Textor also recorded incidents of northeastern trishaw riders who were cheated of sums of money by Bangkok-based riders. Disillusioned with the unions, these riders opted to stay out of them, which meant that welfare programmes fostered by the unions were designed primarily for trishaw riders who were Bangkok residents. In Yogyakarta, Kartodirdjo noted in his survey that working as a trishaw driver was not satisfying for most of his respondents. Out of 250 riders, 184 of them would stop work if other jobs were available. About 76 per cent of these 184 riders wanted to quit as their income was too small while another 30 per cent wanted to do so due to old age or ill-health. Interestingly, a further 21 per cent wanted to quit as trishaw riders because they felt ashamed to occupy such a position in the lower strata of society. Of these 184 riders, the majority preferred to be either traders or 'any occupation' because these were better than trishaw riding (Kartodirdjo 1981:56–57). In a survey of 154 trishaw riders in Penang, about 51 per cent of them were 'dissatisfied' with their jobs with regard to income and occupation despite the fact that the standard of living in Penang at the time was lower than Kuala Lumpur and Johore Bahru. Yet, about 63 per cent of those 'satisfied' with trishaw riding still wanted to quit as they saw a bleak future ahead. Of those who wanted to change their occupation, about 29 per cent preferred to go into business, followed by 26 per cent who wanted a factory job, while another 12 per cent were interested in agriculture. The report urged the Malaysian government to re-train these trishaw riders, 'emplacing them in land scheme projects or giving them easy credit terms to start their business' (Socio-Economic Research and Central Planning Unit 1979:18).

While commerce and agriculture remained appealing to trishaw riders in Southeast Asia, the situation was very different in Singapore. Many trishaw riders were ex-rickshaw pullers who, despite the changing urban landscape, chose to continue riding the trishaw rather than switch to other traders. Unfortunately for them, by the 1970s it had become increasingly difficult for trishaw riders to eke out a living. Younger, healthier riders or those with other jobs in mind left the trade. Only older men were left behind to continue on since they had nowhere else to go to seek a livelihood. Despite the hardship and despair, in many cases they continued riding trishaws up to the time of their deaths. By 1971, many riders could not even pay the subscription fees of the SHTRA (Nanyang Daxue Lishi Xi 1971:51).

Trishaws and the authorities

The trishaw industry absorbed unskilled labour that would otherwise have nowhere else to go. Despite being a popular local means of transport, the industry in Southeast Asia faced a bleak future because it had to contend with unsympathetic modernising governments keen to force these vehicles off the streets. Since the late 1950s, there was the perennial question in each Southeast Asian city of whether or not trishaws should be abolished. Case and Latchford observed that, with the exception of Chiang Mai, the trishaw industry had virtually collapsed throughout Southeast Asia where they claimed as early as 1981 that trishaws were no longer being constructed and there seemed to be no role for them in the future (Case & Latchford 1981:9). Governments in Southeast Asia had taken different measures to ensure that the industry would not survive. In Thailand, the authorities stopped issuing new licenses to trishaw riders in Bangkok from July 1952 and banned the entry of the trishaws into the city from 1 January 1960. However, there was no study of the *consequences* (if any) of the government ban on trishaw riders. Instead, Textor simply assumed that 'the ex-pedicab driver can sometimes be an asset' towards providing leadership in his home village in northeast Thailand (Textor 1961:46). In Jakarta, the trishaws were gradually abolished after being denied entry into particular areas during the day. Trishaw riders also complained of 'inhuman treatment' by government officials with instructions to dispose of the city's trishaws (*Inside Indonesia* 1990:11). In the first two months of 1984 alone, 983 trishaws were removed from streets in south Jakarta and dumped. The ex-riders were then offered a choice between enrolment in a training programme, transmigration to another city, or sent back to their home village (Murray 1991:91–92). Many trishaw riders responded by simply continuing to ride until they were caught. In Surabaya, the introduction of buses in the late 1970s replaced the motorised trishaws that were introduced a decade earlier. The motorised trishaws, in turn, had been introduced in order to get the cycle trishaws off the streets! No new licenses were introduced in Surabaya from 1973 and by 1979 trishaws were reduced to cruising at night only (Pendakur 1984:10–12, 29–31). In Singapore, both the Municipal Council in the mid-1950s and the People's Action Party (PAP) government in 1974 prohibited trishaws from entering certain roads in the city during peak hours.

Furthermore, governments in Southeast Asia employed foreign consultants to improve the state of urban transport. Dick and Rimmer noted that these 'experts' were predominantly British, Americans, Australians, Japanese and Germans. Naturally, these foreign consultants rejected the 'unfamiliar pedicabs' and regarded the trishaws as 'hindrances to smooth traffic flow and took little account of their very real, but less visible, advantages'. The overall consequence was that various Southeast Asian cities came to depend increasingly on foreign technology, capital and skills to develop urban transport – what Dick and Rimmer called an 'imperialism of urban public transport' (Dick & Rimmer 1986:178–187).

Not only did government officials feel compelled to force trishaws off city streets but certain sectors of the general population shared a similar view as well. In Penang, for instance, a minority of passengers interviewed would like to see trishaws banned. The most common reason for this viewpoint was that trishaws 'cause more traffic jam (sic)'. Still others considered them 'unsafe' and 'slow' (Socio-Economic Research and Central Planning Unit

1979:28). In addition, Replogle observed that the technocrats and social elites favoured motorisation as a sign of modernisation and therefore chose to ignore non-motorised modes of transport in their urban transport planning. He noted the lack of diversity in transport in Southeast Asian cities but was obviously misinformed with respect to cycle vehicles in some areas. He claimed that people paid higher travelling costs with the introduction of motorised transport (Replogle 1989:641–642). Yet in Thailand, cycle trishaw fares were more expensive than that of the 'midget-sized' taxis. In Surabaya, the fares of the *bajaj* (small motorised vehicles) were dearer than those of the trishaws.

The various governments' attempts to force trishaws off the roads reflected the debate as to whether or not they should be abolished. If a ban on trishaws occurred, it would result in an increase in unemployment as well as a loss of personalised inner city transport for particular customers such as the elderly and the poor. As early as 1956, it was argued that 'replacement of hard physical work through mechanisation is no more an unmixed blessing here than it has been elsewhere' and that the most obvious result was mass unemployment (Wilson 1956:72). Meier noted that governments in the region were keen to phase out trishaws on the pretext that they were 'inhumane' or 'a hazard to traffic' but he argued that what governments really meant was that 'the tricycles (sic) are a hazard to the autos belonging to the wealthy' (Meier 1977:58). In Indonesia, national leaders such as Sukarno and Ali Sadikin were 'embarrassed and irritated by the masses of the poor who failed to live up to their image of the city' (Abeyasekere 1985:13). Sukarno also condemned the presence of trishaws in 1962. In Yogyakarta, a shift to motorised trishaws would deprive 14–40 persons of jobs for every new vehicle since this could displace 15–40 cycle trishaws (Kartodirdjo 1981:116–117). In November 1976, a project was commenced in Surabaya to replace 40,000 trishaws with 10,000 *bajaj* over five years. Many *bajaj* drivers were not former trishaw riders although, in theory, one out of every four trishaw riders displaced by the *bajaj* was meant to be a driver of a *bajaj*. Dick opined that 'it will be many years yet' before the demand for labour and real wages rise sufficiently for the trishaws to die out of their own accord (Dick 1981a; Dick 1981b:78–79 & 85).

Another frequently used excuse to clear city streets of trishaws was that they were responsible for many vehicle accidents along the roads. However, in Rimmer's analysis of trishaw enterprises in Penang in 1976, he noted that the creation of one-way streets meant trishaws could operate in both directions without disrupting traffic. Furthermore, according to Royal Malaysian Police, only 1.1 per cent of total casualties in 1973 and 1974 were trishaw riders (Rimmer 1978:203). In Textor's survey of trishaw riders in Bangkok, he noted that most accidents involving trishaw riders occurred because the riders failed to look back over their shoulders for oncoming traffic. However, Textor remarked that 'it would be irksome to look back over one's shoulder several hundred times a day' (Textor 1961:18).

Banning trishaws would also mean the end of door-to-door service for mainly middle-income families and the urban poor. The trishaws in Yogyakarta offered high quality service since there was no waiting time and the riders provided a 'personalised' door-to-door service. A trishaw could travel up to six kilometres on average in 30 to 60 minutes (Kartodirdjo 1981:116). In a survey in Penang among trishaw passengers, about 38 per cent of passengers found trishaw service to be 'convenient' and another 33 per cent thought that it was 'easier to obtain' than other forms of transport (Socio-Economic Research and Central Planning Unit 1979:28). Frequent users of trishaws were local residents who were identified as housewives, clerks, sales and related workers, professional and managerial workers, businessmen and the unemployed (Socio-Economic Research and Central Planning Unit 1979:29). In Ujung Pandang, Forbes found that the trishaws were used more frequently by middle-income groups rather than the urban poor because of the fare structure. Furthermore, there were trishaws employed by families on a regular basis to send children off to school or to escort women to and from markets or houses of relatives (Forbes 1978:220–221). Forbes concluded that:

> The trishaw rider is able to cater specifically to the needs of the wealthy and this accounts for both the large number of riders and their comparatively expensive fares. He offers transport door-to-door, but more importantly he offers security to his passengers in a city which quite unjustifiably in my view, is thought a dangerous place to travel unescorted (Forbes 1979:250).

Despite the obvious provision of good transport service in many cities, the governments in the region still wanted trishaws off the streets as soon as possible. It seems that 'the march of progress is inexorable' and hence 'if the road and transport systems were to be improved to cater to the traffic load, the *beca* [trishaws] have to go in favour of motorized transport' (Khoo 1981:22).

A SLOW RIDE INTO THE PAST

Reflections on the industry in Southeast Asia

In 1998, James Scott depicted the failure of government schemes to improve human livelihood in his picture of a 'high modernist' state (Scott 1998). An element of the 'high modernist' state was the intention of various governments to re-plan and rebuild various cities in order to engineer changes in social life and attitudes of the people. He considered such plans to be 'great state-sponsored calamities' planned by politicians and administrators who harboured 'grandiose and utopian plans' for the country (Scott 1998:89). He cites examples from Iran under the Shah before he was deposed, 'villagization' in Vietnam, city planning in Brasilia and Chandigargh and the utopian ideals of Nazi Germany.

As the countries in Southeast Asia began rebuilding their economy and society with the end of World War II, it is evident that 'high modernist' ideals had set in. Engineers, planners, administrators, politicians, technocrats, architects and anyone else involved in the planning, construction and policy-making of key cities across the region were imbued with similar ideals of 'modernity'. The cities should have well-planned roads, old buildings should be demolished and new ones erected and urban transportation had to be improved. With these ideals in mind, the trishaws in the region became an anomaly. Those involved with city planning and administration were determined to improve public transport by putting more buses and taxis on the roads while banning trishaws from certain streets in the city centre or (in the case of Bangkok) banning them altogether. Foreign planners and engineers were employed by the authorities in the region in order to 'modernise' the cities. Since these consultants were not from the region, they showed a lack of understanding of the needs of the urban poor and used their understanding of how foreign cities were organised to 'modernise' Southeast Asian cities. In their eyes, anything that was indigenous was not 'modern' and should be sidelined.

This chapter on cycle transport in Southeast Asia shows that, despite the attempts by the authorities to push them to the fringes of urban society, the trishaws remained for a time an important means of public transport for large sections of society, especially the urban poor. The trishaw riders provided door-to-door service for their passengers that bus and taxi drivers could not do. Many of the riders in Southeast Asia had little or no education and some of them were even living in abject squalor. Trishaw riding became an occupational option for them precisely because it required no prior knowledge or skill. Nonetheless, trishaw riding was hard labour and the surveys conducted showed that if they had a choice, the riders would pick another job. As time passed, the authorities in the region began to implement urban renewal policies that had a great impact on the lives of the trishaw riders. Suddenly, a key mode of public transport was denounced as 'obsolete' and 'unsafe', blamed for causing traffic chaos and held responsible for vehicle accidents along the roads. The city and national authorities in the region began to marginalise the trishaw industry either by benign neglect or by introducing policies that would lead to a reduction in the number of trishaws – if not an outright ban on them. Public perception of what was deemed to be a 'respectable' job also worked to the disadvantage of the trishaw riders, as they were seen – like the rickshaw pullers in the first half of the twentieth century – to be nothing more than 'beasts of burden'.

Chapter 2

THE ADVENT OF THE TRISHAWS

The introduction of trishaws

Trishaws first appeared on the streets of Singapore in April 1914. The initial venture was modest; only 15 were introduced by an unknown syndicate. The fare was the same as first-class rickshaws – six cents per mile and an additional 2.5 cents per mile or part thereof (SMAR 1914:2; Sim 1975:7; Warren 1986:77).[1] These first 'pedal-rickshaws' were crudely assembled, consisting of chairs bolted to tricycle frames. These novel vehicles did not last very long on the streets and all 15 were soon sold and sent to Java. An American company expressed interest in introducing 500 'improved' trishaws later that year but there is no mention made of the application in the Registrar of Vehicles Office report for 1915 (SMAR 1914:2). In 1936, the Municipal Commission turned down proposals to register and license trishaws on the grounds that they were a traffic menace. The commissioners argued that, 'it will probably take some time before the riders of trishas acquire the road sense which is necessary for the safety of road users' (NAS, NA 441, MPMCS, Minutes of the Additional Meeting of the Committee Numbers 1 & 3, 16.10.1946).[2]

Following the British surrender on 15 February 1942, the Japanese Military Administration renamed the island Syonan-To ('Light of the South'). Trishaws began to re-appear on the city streets during the Japanese Occupation (NAS, MHA 445, R of S 181/47, 20.04.1946).[3] Rickshaws were

---

[1]   Sim, however, did not mention what happened to the trishaws between 1914 and 1942, if they existed then.

[2]   It was the President of the Municipal Commission who made the comment. 'Trishas' was the old term used for trishaws.

[3]   On 20 April 1946, Quek Yew Boey, Vice-President of the Singapore Trishaw Owners Association (STOA), wrote to the Registrar of Societies that the STOA did not exist prior

THE ADVENT OF THE TRISHAWS

still a popular mode of transport for ordinary people in Singapore and the trishaw was a logical combination of a bicycle and the rickshaw. Some local historians date the first appearance of trishaws to 1944 (Qiu 1990:93). In point of fact, the trishaw had to be introduced as a novel form of transport during the Japanese Occupation. Petrol was scarce; any new vehicle introduced in the streets of Syonan-To that did not require petrol would certainly be welcomed by the Japanese administrators. Furthermore, the Japanese themselves had requisitioned many motor vehicles on the island. It was left to the trishaw to provide a transport service, and this vehicle was precisely what the Japanese had in mind in solving transport shortage (NAS, A000358/09, reel 5). On 8 July 1942, *The Syonan Times* reported that 'with the object of alleviating the present transport difficulties, the former restriction [by the British] on the number of rickshas and tricycles have (sic) been lifted'. The newspaper also noted that 'a novel transport vehicle will be introduced in the city by next month'. The new vehicle was called the 'rickshacycle', and was described as 'a contraption very much like a tricycle except that there will be two seats for passengers by the side of the driver's seat'. The Registrar of Vehicles proposed that a roof or awning be fitted on the new vehicle to protect passengers from the rain. The new vehicle could eventually replace the rickshaws as a popular means of transport (*The Syonan Times*, 08.07.1942).

It was reported that 'as further proof that the tricycle-ricksha is proving itself popular among the Syonan public', ten more vehicles were introduced which brought the total number of trishaws available for hire to 48. The newspaper noted that what made the trishaw popular were the cheaper fare and its faster speed against the rickshaw (*The Syonan Times*, 19.09.1942). *The Syonan Times* also reported that one Sunny Tan of Balestier Road had designed a new trishaw 'which represents the last word in streamlining'. These trishaws were meant only for private use and built to give comfort to the trishaw rider. Sunny Tan constructed three models of the new trishaw – the men's sports, the women's sports and the touring models, although the newspaper did not describe how the models differed from each other. The cost of the new trishaw depended on the fittings and the cheapest was priced at $300. Sunny Tan wanted the new vehicles to be leased, with the purchaser paying a third of the cost and the balance to be settled by monthly instalments (*The Syonan Times*, 08.10.1942).

---

to 1941 'as at that time *there were no trishaws in existence and moreover the Municipality of Singapore did not approve of this type of transport*' (emphasis added).

A SLOW RIDE INTO THE PAST

Riding the trishaw during the Japanese Occupation

The presence of large numbers of trishaws in Japanese-occupied Singapore eased the pressure on the Japanese Military Administration for public transport on the island. Cycling the trishaw was also a novel experience for the riders not only in physical terms but also with the fear that came from picking up Japanese military personnel as passengers. Chia Kee Huat remembered that although rickshaw pullers were still running in the streets, trishaw riding proved more popular. It was easier riding a trishaw than pulling a rickshaw. He remembered that the Japanese military were the most difficult passengers. The Japanese soldiers were based in military camps in the interior of the island and they expected the trishaw riders to travel such long distances after a night out in the city. The soldiers also decided how much the ride was worth! Furthermore, the trishaw riders would find it difficult to return to the city area. En route to the city, they could meet other Japanese soldiers who wanted a trip back to the camps. Chia, however, noticed that the Japanese soldiers would alight from the trishaws at a distance from the camp entrance; he suspected that it was to prevent their officers from seeing them arrive at the camp in a trishaw (NAS, A000358/09, reels 5 & 6). The officers had expected their men to walk back to camp.

In order to avoid picking up Japanese soldiers, the trishaw riders would work until 8 or 9 pm. After the screening of the last show in the cinemas, people would gradually stream out. The trishaw riders would rush to pick up cinema goers, many of whom lived in the city area. Chia remembered that they had to do this in order to avoid being hailed by the Japanese soldiers. That, however, might not work at times. Chia remembered Japanese soldiers lying in wait for trishaw riders. When one rode by, they would ambush the poor trishaw rider, threaten him with a sword and force him to give the soldiers a ride (NAS, A000358/09, reel 5). Tay Meng Hock also recalled taking a trishaw during the Japanese Occupation:

> [I came across Japanese sentries], you see, when I bought some raw materials from a chemical company. And in those days, you know, I usually dress up with a [pair of] white shorts, white shirt, and I usually carry a briefcase. So I sat in a trishaw, put the goods on the floorboard. And when the trishaw was passing along [the] Raffles Institution gate down there, the Japanese sentry thought I was a Japanese officer. So the moment they saw me passing that way, the two of them stood up, you

know, and saluted me, you know. So I had to respond by saluting back to the Japanese officers (NAS, A000470/10, reel 7).

Consequently, Tay did not pass by the same place again for fear of being arrested for impersonating a Japanese officer.

The presence of the trishaw marked an increased rivalry with the older rickshaws. An early case of a fight between a trishaw rider and a rickshaw puller over who had the right to pick up a passenger took place during the Japanese Occupation. A rickshaw puller was about to pick up a passenger when the trishaw rider pulled up and offered the same passenger a ride. A fight ensued and eight other rickshaw pullers came to the assistance of their fellow puller in assaulting the trishaw rider. The trishaw rider, in self-defence, picked up a piece of concrete and struck the puller. The trishaw rider was subsequently fined $100 for causing hurt to the rickshaw puller 'under grave and sudden provocation'. Both men were also ordered to pay a bond of $100 each and 'to keep the peace' for six months (*The Syonan Times*, 20.09.1942).

Recognition of wartime trishaw deposits

The Japanese surrender at City Hall on 12 September 1945 brought to an end almost four years of war and utter misery in East and Southeast Asia, and the beginning of the British Military Administration (BMA) in Singapore that lasted until 1 April 1946. The British soon recognised the presence of the trishaws on the island when they returned:

> One innovation which the Japanese introduced, or permitted to be introduced, was the trishaw...This had largely replaced the former rickshaw and subsequently, the British Civil authorities gave it their blessing, discrediting the rickshaw in its favour (Gilmour 1950: 121–122).

Chia Kee Huat remembered that during the BMA, British, French and American military personnel were on the island. His impression was that the American sailors were a generous lot. After a short ride, the Americans could give $10 to the rider – a huge sum in 1945. When passengers were charged in increments of 10 cents, the American sailors were calculating their fare in increments of $1 (NAS, A000358/09, reel 9)!

The promulgation of the BMA, however, meant new troubles for the trishaw riders on the island. With the end of the Japanese Occupation, the riders faced new regulations and demands when the British returned. All assets and properties of the Japanese were seized by the Custodian of Property. At least one company named Siroki Sangyo KK had sold trishaws to interested parties during the Japanese Occupation after the trishaw riders had paid a $250 deposit. Nothing else is known about this company, however, except that they kept the deposits until the end of the Japanese Occupation. Now the assets of the Siroki Sangyo KK were seized by the Custodian of Property, including the deposits paid by the riders who had purchased their vehicles from the company.

The BMA period was also the first time the trishaw owners and riders faced government attempts to regulate the industry. On 30 September 1945, a representative of the Singapore Tricycle Mutual Workers Association wrote to the BMA with four requests. First, the association asked that the deposits with the Syonan Trishaw Association be recognised by the Custodian of Property. Secondly, the association requested that an estimated price be placed on trishaws sold to potential riders. Thirdly, assistance should be given to the Road Transport Department (RTD) on the renewal of trishaw licenses. Lastly, the association hoped that trishaws detained by the RTD would be returned to the rightful owners (NAS, NA 878, BMA 12/46, 30.09.1945). The letter was passed to the Chinese Affairs Secretariat who referred the matter to the Custodian of Property with the comment that 'the request generally seems to be reasonable' (NAS, NA 878, BMA 12/46, 01.10.1945 & 31.10.1945).

The Custodian of Property, however, was less sympathetic. In his reply, he mentioned that a Special Manager had been appointed to round up about 300 trishaws and have them registered by the RTD. Registered trishaws would be made available for public use after 15 October, and it was then possible for the Tricycle Mutual Workers Association to purchase these vehicles. The Custodian of Property opined that 'any deposit made with any previous Japanese association does not concern me'; what he was interested in was whether the association would be willing to purchase any of these 300 trishaws (NAS, NA 878, BMA 12/46, 03.10.1945).

The association was dismayed and sent a deputation to the Chinese Affairs Secretariat on 31 October, with two appeals. The association hoped that the BMA could acknowledge the payment of the $250 deposit as it was money earned 'through the blood and sweat of the pullers'. The association also called on the BMA to acknowledge 'the rightful owners' of the trishaws

THE ADVENT OF THE TRISHAWS

(NAS, NA 878, BMA 12/46, 31.10.1945). The trishaw riders were using vehicles only with permission from the Custodian of Property. Yet, since the vehicles were enemy property, the Custodian could easily seize them and have them sold. Those trishaw riders who paid $250 during the Japanese Occupation would now be without a vehicle. After the meeting, even the Chinese Affairs Secretariat concluded that 'Government should respond by a big gesture and let these people have the trishaws as if they had been properly purchased' (NAS, NA 878, BMA 12/46, 31.10.1945).

In a reply that came typically from a department in the civil service, the Chief Staff Officer of the BMA ordered the Custodian of Property to sell the trishaws for $1 each to the Tricycle Mutual Workers Association if the latter could produce documentary proof that deposits of $250 per vehicle had been paid during the Japanese Occupation. This was a conciliatory gesture towards the trishaw riders. The response from the association, however, showed that the Chief Staff Officer was clueless on financial transactions during the war years. Two representatives from the association had to tell him, on 10 November 1945, that 'we are unable to give you the receipts for the money which we paid to the Japanese firm Shorokie Trishaw Co. [that is, Siroki Sangyo] as that firm never issued receipts per payments received (sic)'. However, the association would vouch for all payments made during the Japanese Occupation (NAS, NA 878, BMA 12/45, 10.11.1945).

No response came from the Chief Staff Officer but the BMA eventually backed down from its demand to the association to produce receipts. The association compiled a list of 309 trishaw riders on 9 November for the Chinese Affairs Secretariat, along with the Siroki Sangyo KK registration number and the riders' own trishaw number. After the Chinese Affairs Secretariat confirmed the list, the fee was collected and passed to the Custodian of Property, who decided to close the matter by accepting payment of $1 per rider 'to square my books'. The next day, a single receipt for $309 was issued to the Siroki Sangyo KK even though the company had disappeared (NAS, NA 878, BMA 12/46, 09.11.1945, 13.11.1945 & 14.11.1945). On 15 November, a second list of 12 riders was submitted by the association to the Chinese Affairs Secretariat, and the names of another three riders were presented on 17 November. The Custodian of Property issued a single receipt of $15 on 23 November. The matter had finally come to a close, although two more trishaw riders had to pay $1 each in February and April 1946 to keep their trishaws.

Furthermore, the association asked the Chinese Affairs Secretariat on 10 November for permission to be given by the RTD to the association to issue trishaw licenses instead, so as 'to save large numbers of people' going to the RTD. The association also asked the police – through the Chinese Secretariat – if they could appoint a single representative to deal with the police directly in cases where traffic summonses were issued against association members. The Chinese Affairs Secretariat was to find out later that the association never followed up this issue with the police (NAS, NA 878, BMA 12/46, 10.11.1945 & 29.11.1945). However, the Controller of Road Transport did not intend to transfer the issuing of licenses from the RTD 'as this would give the Association a monopoly'. The fear was that the association 'would force all trishaw owners to be members of their association whether they wanted to or not'. The RTD insisted that it was 'quite capable' of issuing the trishaw licenses (NAS, NA 878, BMA 12/46, 19.11.1945).

Arbitrary increase of licence fees

Another problem that arose from the end of World War II was the sudden increase in licence fees imposed on the trishaw riders by unscrupulous trishaw owners. The first complaint was filed by a 'Trishaw Association' to the Chinese Affairs Secretariat on 11 January 1946. Some owners were charging the riders as much as $18 for the renewal of licences when the fee was fixed by the authorities at $7.50. (NAS, NA 878, BMA 12/46, 12.01.1946). The representatives of the Trishaw Association alleged that one such individual known to arbitrarily increase the trishaw licence fee was Ban Hoe Leong of 15 Nankin Street just outside Chinatown. During the Japanese Occupation, he had purchased about 100 trishaws, and then 'sold' a few to some riders who were acknowledged as 'shareholders'. It seemed that there was actually no business transaction since the trishaw rider had to provide his own trishaw. Yet, he had to pay Ban $200 for the registration plate and have the trishaw registered under Ban's firm. Furthermore, Ban paid the authorities $7.50 for the renewal of each trishaw licence but subsequently charged each trishaw rider $50. After the Japanese surrender, Ban was still overcharging the riders, but this time 'on a smaller scale', at $15 per trishaw rider. The representatives urged the Chinese Affairs Secretariat to inspect Ban's receipt books (NAS, NA 878, BMA 12/46, 12.01.1946 & 15.01.1946).

The STOA, however, disputed the claims made by the 'Trishaw Association'. They approached Rodyk & Davidson – a major law firm still in existence today – who sent a letter to the Chinese Affairs Secretariat, explaining that the practice of issuing trishaw licences was similar to that of the pre-war registration of rickshaws. Rickshaw owners were given licences by the Municipal Vehicles Department (predecessor of the RTD), and these licences were then distributed to the pullers. The same practice for trishaws meant that there was a possibility that the number of trishaws owned by the owners might not be the same as the number of licences issued. An unlicensed owner may register his trishaw under the name of the actual owner (the licensee). The licensee, however, was responsible for all registration and inspection of trishaws (NAS, NA 878, BMA 12/46, 14.01.1946). Once an association representing the interests of the trishaw riders was established, however, the owners feared that the riders would register their vehicles in the latter's names when the vehicles were called up for inspection and registration. The STOA argued that as they were the authorised licensee, the RTD should continue to work with them in the registration of trishaws. The STOA also accused the 'Trishaw Association' of issuing instructions to riders and unlicensed owners not to approach the STOA for inspection and registration of trishaws. This matter, however, was not taken up by the Secretary for Chinese Affairs as it was not under his purview.

Rodyk & Davidson noted that it was only a matter of time before all trishaws had to be inspected for registration and payment of licence fees. Therefore, members of the STOA would have to recall all their trishaws for this purpose. The STOA also accused the 'Trishaw Association' of hindering its efforts by issuing instructions to trishaw riders to register their trishaws under their own names, so as to prevent the licensees from rightfully taking back the vehicles. The STOA was not in favour of the RTD doing the registration of trishaws, as 'it will entail a greater volume of work' for the department. It was easier for the department to deal with the licensees directly rather than each individual trishaw rider (NAS, NA 878, BMA 12/46, 14.01.1946).

Eventually the representatives of the 'Trishaw Association' went to the RTD on 15 January 1946 and three requests from the association were approved. First, all trishaws purchased by members of the association from the STOA would be registered as belonging to the trishaw riders. Secondly, all registration of trishaws belonging to members of the association would be recorded by the association. Finally, the RTD advised the representatives to approach the STOA for receipts of any sales of trishaws to the trishaw riders. If receipts could not be produced, the association should write to a legal firm and the RTD for permission to view the ledger books of the STOA. The RTD would arrange a meeting for this to be done (NAS, NA 878, BMA 12/46, 15.01.1946).

Issue of trishaw licences

In February 1946, problems regarding the issue of trishaw licences surfaced when the Tricycle Mutual Workers Association sent an appeal to the Chinese Affairs Secretariat. The association had applied for 200 licenses on 1 February and was informed by the Registrar of Vehicles to prepare the vehicles for inspection. These vehicles were constructed after the trishaw riders had borrowed money from various sources. However, the Registrar informed the association on 13 February that only 60 new licenses would be issued. On 18 February, the association brought 20 trishaws to be inspected, and 15 passed. The association also charged that most trishaws that came from Hock Hin, a firm that acted as an agent for trishaws, passed the inspection. It was alleged that the agent paid for the licenses without the trishaws being present for inspection but trishaws sent by members of the association for inspection were rejected. In other words, the association accused the RTD of sloppy inspections or worse, corruption.

The Secretary for Chinese Affairs redirected the letter to the RTD with the message that 'so far this Association has behaved in a correct manner in the dealings with me', and therefore, 'I feel disposed to help it as far as possible'. A few days later, one Anthony Chia from the association asked for a meeting with a Senior Officer of the Department. The Registrar of Vehicles not only did not arrange for a meeting but also told the association that 'there are only 60 odd licenses available to reach the limit allowed for hire sanrinshaw [trishaw]' and that 'every individual should produce his sanrinshaw for registration at this office and preference will be given according to priority' (NAS, NA 878, BMA 12/46, 22.02.1946, 25.02.1946 & 26.02.1946). The association appealed to the Secretary for Chinese Affairs again on 28 February. Of the 60 licenses available, the association was given 30. But the association also charged that while they were given an allotted 15 new licenses on 18 February, the Controller of Road Transport issued more than 300 licenses to 'monopolised license-holders' (in other words, the trishaw owners). Representatives of the association, however, met the Controller of Road Transport on 27 February and the Association was told the next day that there were 23 more trishaw licenses up for grabs. The association sent 23 new trishaws and secured all 23 licenses.

Yet this was not enough. Members of the association had constructed 200 new trishaws but the association had only managed to secure 53 licenses. To members of the association this was a significant loss because it meant that while they had the *means* of living – the trishaws – they could not make use of this means since no licenses were issued. The association suggested to the Secretary for Chinese Affairs that all licenses issued to trishaws that once belonged to the Japanese or that were held jointly by Japanese and Chinese owners be transferred to members of the association. The association was concerned that, should individual riders not be given the licenses, they would need to hire the vehicles from the trishaw owners. The association made a rough calculation of riders' expenses. Firstly, the rider would need to pay $100 to the trishaw owner for a license; the trishaw would then be registered under the name of the owner. Secondly, because the trishaw was registered in the name of the owner, the rider needed to fork out $20 to $30 for any transfer of ownership; alternatively, if ownership hadn't been transferred into the name of the rider, the rider had to pay the owner $1.50 rent per day for riding the vehicle. And lastly, all expenses for repairs would be borne by the trishaw rider. The association, frustrated with these issues, looked to the Secretary for Chinese Affairs for assistance.

In the end, a compromise was reached. Agreements had to be signed between owners and the riders. Under these agreements, the owners who held the licenses would entrust the riders with the vehicles; the vehicles would have been registered with the RTD; and the trishaw riders now had the right to ride the vehicles. However, should the trishaw rider decide to let another rider ride the vehicle, the former had to get consent from the owner. The owner would then issue a new agreement with the second rider. A sample agreement was produced by Anthony Chia when he met the Controller of Road Transport, and this was signed by Wang Ah See (a trishaw rider) and Teo Moh Seng of Hock Leong Hin Trishaw Singapore (a trishaw owner).

Alleged malpractice by trishaw owners

In March 1946 the Singapore Tricycle Workers Mutual Help Association brought a complaint against trishaw owners to the attention of the Secretary for Chinese Affairs. On 26 March the association complained about an alleged malpractice by Chin Shen Tricycle. The trishaw company had allegedly forged licenses that had been distributed to trishaw riders – the association had found that trishaws with registration numbers 2929 and 3727 were each sold to two men. Furthermore, a trishaw bearing the registration number 3506 was sold to a trishaw rider, but the number was not stamped on the vehicle. Lastly, another trishaw, bearing the registration number 3712, was reported missing by a rider on 30 January that year, but the association soon learnt that a trishaw bearing the same registration number was located in Chin Shen Tricycle. The situation was compounded further when the association complained that trishaw riders were beaten up by the owners when the former demanded that 'trishaw papers' (in other words, the registration papers) be issued by the latter in order to have the vehicles transferred to the names of the individual riders.

On 1 July 1946, the association wrote about this matter to ECS Adkins, the new Secretary for Chinese Affairs. All six trishaws mentioned in the association's letter of 26 March had apparently been seized by the Beach Road Police Station, pending an investigation into any wrongdoing by Chin Shen Tricycle. Statements from eight trishaw riders concerning the six vehicles were also recorded for Adkins. The matter was closed and the trishaws subsequently returned to the riders on 10 July.

It seemed that trishaw registration number 2929 was purchased by Wong Chung in 1944. On 15 January 1946, the proprietor of Chin Shen Tricycle asked Wong to bring his trishaw license plate and to collect it back in a week's time. Wong tried to see the proprietor later but did not get to do so until 19 March, and the proprietor gave him a license plate bearing the number 3712. The receipt showing the sale of license number 2929 was then destroyed by the proprietor, who told Wong that the registration number 2929 had been cancelled and that 3712 was a new number. Puzzled, Wong sought the help of the association and was advised to write to the Secretary for Chinese Affairs. The secretary gave Wong a letter to be passed to the Registrar of Vehicles. When Wong reached the Registrar's office, another trishaw bearing the registration number 2929 appeared. Seah Ing Teng had purchased his trishaw from Chin Shen Tricycle on 10 November 1945, and the vehicle was sold to him bearing the registration number 2929. At the Registrar's office, Wong was informed that trishaw number 3712 had been reported missing.

The complex matter was eventually cleared up. Seah's trishaw retained the number 2929. Wong's trishaw, however, now bore the number 3712. The trishaw rider who reported his vehicle missing – Lim Kwee Soon – corrected an error and reported that his trishaw license number was actually 3721. Yeow Ah Khiok – who had owned trishaw license number 3712 – was allowed to keep his vehicle (but perhaps with a change in the license number). The vehicle had been seized by the Beach Road Police Station since Lim had given the wrong number. As for the two trishaws bearing the same number 3727 that were purchased from Chin Shen Tricycle, an inspector at the Registrar's office allowed one of the trishaw riders named

Kang Pia Chwee to keep the number 3727. Another number was issued by the inspector for the trishaw owned by Chua Kum Choon. Lastly, the license plate number for Quek Ah Yow's trishaw was confirmed to be 3506.

Transition from rickshaw to trishaw

The problems with the nascent industry outlined so far could be attributed to the general administrative problems the British had to face when they returned to Singapore. These problems and the confusion that occurred within the industry in the immediate post-war years, however, were overshadowed by more important events. Of greater significance to the trishaw industry in post-war Singapore was the escalating movement to ban rickshaws from the island. The movement was evidently part of a worldwide one, with the main reason given being the 'degrading' treatment of rickshaw pullers as 'beasts of burden'. In 1928 it was predicted that, with an increase in the number of motorcars in the roads of Shanghai, rickshaws would 'ultimately be driven out of business' (*China Weekly Review*, 01.12.1928:4). By 1934, it was suggested that the rickshaws would not be banned in Shanghai because 'that would interfere with the racketeering owners of the ricsha-companies, who earn big profits by forcing men to perform the work of dumb animals or gasoline-propelled vehicles' (*China Weekly Review*, 03.03.1934:1). The rickshaw was seen as 'contrary to the spirit of modernism' and that it could be 'eliminated just as naturally as horse-carriages were replaced by automobiles' (*China Weekly Review*, 07.04.1934:214). In 1946, the National Government of China opted to abolish the rickshaw in Nanjing and Shanghai within two years. An American-owned newspaper, the *Shanghai Evening Post*, condemned that decision, arguing instead that 'the ricksha puller is often one of the most rugged of individualists, and any degradation about his lot seems to reside exclusively in the mind of the sentimentalist' (*Singapore Free Press*, 05.08.1946). This attitude among Western commentators did not exist in Singapore as the city prepared to embark on that same course.

When Singapore came under the dominion of the Union Jack once again in August 1945, there were increasing calls to ban rickshaws on humanitarian grounds. The first cry to ban these vehicles on these grounds had occurred as early as 1926, when the need for rickshaws was publicly questioned with the increased number of motor buses available. Since these buses also operated in the outlying districts, the city became overcrowded with rickshaws from the suburbs and rural areas. It forced the Registrar of Vehicles to seriously consider the issue of abolition since 'road space in the city was at a premium' (Nanyang Daxue Lishi Xi 1971:6–7; Warren 1986:100). The argument posed was that rickshaw pulling was inhumane since it represented as a form of labour a great loss of human dignity. However, the abolition question and the associated issue of humanitarian concerns remained unanswered until the end of the Japanese Occupation. According to Rajabali Jumabhoy, a Municipal Commissioner from the end of the war until 1948:

> After the war, there was some higher regard for self-respect in the community. And we thought it is inhuman and degrading that a person, a human being, should pull a rickshaw as a traffic convenience. Besides this, after the war there was an increase of motor vehicles and it was not always safe for a rickshaw to run about the streets (NAS, Transcript of A000074/37:94).

Furthermore, as trishaws were increasingly seen in the city streets, the Municipal Commission could plan a ban of the rickshaws and build up the nascent trishaw industry at the same time.

On 12 July 1946, the Commission first proposed that all licences for rickshaws not be renewed when they expired (NAS, NA 441, MPMCS, Minutes of a General Committee Meeting, 12.07.1946; *The Straits Times*, 23.07.1946). However, the Acting Secretary of Chinese Affairs, after meeting a representative of the Singapore Rickshaw Pullers Mutual Aid Association on 24 July, pointed out that since licenses were renewed every four months, it meant that rickshaws could be abolished as early as 1 September as the next expiry date was 31 August. This proposal could result in 5,000 rickshaw pullers suddenly finding themselves unemployed. Furthermore, a considerable number of them could not take up trishaw riding due to old age and other problems; they already would not be able to take advantage of the proposed issue of 2,000 new trishaw licenses. As a result of the Acting Secretary of Chinese Affairs' intervention, the Municipal Commission voted for only half of all rickshaw licenses – to be determined by a lottery – to be abolished on 31 December 1946 and the remainder to expire on 30 April 1947 (NAS, NA 441, MPMCS, Minutes of a General Committee Meeting, 09.08.1946).

The possible fate and/or role of the rickshaw came to the fore again in a Standing Committee meeting of the Municipal Commission on 16 October 1946. Commissioner DK Walters remarked that rickshaws were 'less objectionable' than trishaws as a traffic hazard when they plied the roads.

THE ADVENT OF THE TRISHAWS

This, he claimed, was a view 'endorsed by several Chinese gentlemen whom he has consulted'. Walters suggested that the number of rickshaw pullers be limited while any further applications for registration of pullers be rejected. He was not in favour of having more trishaws on the streets. For a brief moment it appeared that this argument had won the day, as the President of the Municipal Commission overturned the earlier decision to abolish rickshaws by the end of April 1947. Instead, following another suggestion by Walters, the commissioners agreed to formulate new laws concerning the registration and licensing of pullers and to put a ceiling of 2,198 on rickshaw licenses (MPMCS, Minutes of Meeting of Standing Committees Numbers 1 & 3, 16.10.1946). It was thought that the quick abolition of rickshaws was also an 'inhuman act' towards the pullers who had been plying the streets with their trade for more than 60 years. There was also an inherent belief among members of the public that while trishaws were more comfortable to ride in than the rickshaws, the pullers had better road manners than trishaw riders (*The Straits Times*, 24.10.1946).

However, in a Municipal Commission meeting on 29 November, John Laycock moved a motion that the initial decision to abolish rickshaws by 30 April 1947 be reinstated (NAS, NA 441, MPMCS, Minutes of an Ordinary Meeting, 29.11.1946; *Nanyang Siang Pau*, 30.11.1946). Calling rickshaw pulling 'absolutely degrading', 'inhumanitarian (sic)' and 'obsolete' (*The Straits Times*, 02.11.1946), Laycock outlined his proposal to totally ban rickshaws on three grounds. Firstly, he felt that rickshaws were dangerously slow. From the point of view of motorised traffic, rickshaws simply occupied particular lanes for too long a period of time. He claimed that with the increasing number of motor vehicles, it was progressively difficult for pullers to manoeuvre correctly since, in the face of speeding vehicles, there was a limit to what human labour could endure. Rickshaw pullers, he noted, found it difficult to pull their vehicles up a hill or over long distances. Hence, Laycock felt that both the safety and public effectiveness of the rickshaws in such circumstances were markedly reduced. Secondly, Laycock noted that for humanitarian and health reasons rickshaws could not continue to be supported, as pullers had to work in the outdoors all year round regardless of weather. Many pullers became chronically ill as they ate little and had to forfeit part of whatever meagre income they earned for renting rickshaws. Their poor health tended to result in early death, with tuberculosis as the main cause of morbidity. In the face of such dire circumstances, Laycock encouraged the pullers working at his office – he was a lawyer – to abandon their occupation. His office then paid for the passage tickets and gave some money to the ex-pullers before sending them back to China. The last regular puller working for his office left Singapore in August 1946 (*Nanyang Siang Pau*, 30.11.1946).

The final reason Laycock wanted rickshaws abolished was simply because he felt the occupation constituted a demeaning job for human beings. Furthermore, he noted that it was mainly Chinese who did this work in Singapore and Malaya, which Laycock felt simply reinforced the stereotypical image of the Chinese as a 'defeated' race. The hard question facing many Singaporean Chinese then was why their fellow Chinese should have to continue to be 'beasts of burden' to other nationalities (*The Straits Times*, 02.11.1946). Laycock claimed that rickshaw pulling required immense strength and since it was done mainly by Chinese, it represented and signified a form of public humiliation for all Chinese. He recalled that during the Japanese Occupation, one Caucasian was forced by the Japanese to pull a rickshaw so as to symbolically humiliate the Caucasian. The shame felt by that Caucasian also reflected the shame experienced by the Chinese now, who wondered why a classical civilisation like China would continue to permit its citizens to do such degrading work and remain poverty-stricken for so long. Laycock finished his speech by claiming that the time had come when the Singapore Chinese themselves wanted to ban rickshaws. In what was to be the last Municipal Commission meeting that he would attend, Laycock declared that Singapore 'should place itself firmly in the forefront of social progress and set an example to the older cities of South-East Asia', since it was the 'natural capital' of the entire Malay Archipelago (NAS, ML 1919, LM 267/46).

However, underlying Laycock's rhetoric and alleged humane concern was a more basic motive. He fully understood the traffic situation at that time – there were 4,439 motor cars on the roads, but public transport, especially bus services, remained poor and there were just 1,138 taxis available (ARVRD 1951). Therefore, while he favoured banning rickshaws, he expected them to be replaced by trishaws. He actually moved the motion to have no limit with regards to the licensing of trishaws. In any event, the logic of his arguments to ban rickshaws was flimsy. If rickshaws tended to occupy a traffic lane for too long a period of time, trishaws would do the same. Furthermore, like rickshaw pullers, trishaw riders were also always exposed to the elements. His final reason for the rickshaw ban perhaps was more out of sympathy for the Singapore Chinese, who suffered terribly during the Japanese Occupation. His account of the humiliated Caucasian parallels Low Ngiong Ing's recollection that a Chinese passenger was forced to switch roles with the rickshaw puller as a form of 'Robin Hood-like behaviour' at the behest of the Japanese (Low 1973:7).

THE ADVENT OF THE TRISHAWS

Some commissioners initially disagreed with Laycock's proposal. One of them thought that rickshaw pulling was not immoral and proposed to continue the issuing of licences before abolishing it altogether in two years' time. However, the Vehicles Registration Department (VRD, formerly the RTD) would stop issuing licences when a puller was in poor health or when a rickshaw was in a dilapidated condition. After two years the streets would be cleared of rickshaws and the pullers could switch jobs in a more suitable time (*Nanyang Siang Pau*, 30.11.1946). The President of the Municipal Commission, however, remarked that with the introduction of trishaws during the Occupation, the new vehicle was here to stay. Hence he noted that it was easier to abolish rickshaws so that the pullers could either quit or make the transition to trishaw riding without feeling as much pain over loss of traditional employment (*Sin Chew Jit Poh*, 30.11.1946). Laycock's motion was carried in the end and rickshaws had to go by 30 April 1947.

Laycock's stand and proposal had the full support of the *Nanyang Siang Pau*, one of two leading Chinese newspapers in Singapore. The *Nanyang Siang Pau* was outraged that there were still commissioners who wanted the rickshaws retained any longer. Nor did the paper support the need for a major medical check-up of pullers in order to de-register them since it felt that the rickshawmen could readily switch jobs in the 'informal' sector (*Nanyang Siang Pau*, 30.11.1946). Other major papers took a line which also supported the decision. The *Singapore Free Press* reported that with the ban on rickshaws, there was 'the severance of yet another link with old Singapore', which implied that rickshaws were not a technological sign of urban progress. It also noted that rickshaw owners, now desperate to get rid of their vehicles before 1 May 1947, were willing to sell them for as little as $50 each to anybody willing to purchase a rickshaw. Overnight, the rickshaw became a condemned vehicle and so 'scrapped of the hood, mudguards and licence-plates, it is quite likely that a few will be used in the neighbouring islands to carry firewood and estate produce by villagers' (*Singapore Free Press*, 26.04.1947). *The Malaya Tribune* rejoiced, writing that from 1 May 1947, 'Singaporeans can say proudly that no more human beasts of transport can be seen along the streets' (*The Malaya Tribune*, 01.05.1947). *The Straits Times* called most of the ex-rickshaw pullers 'human wrecks'; many were old, weak and seriously ill, especially from tuberculosis (*The Straits Times*, 03.05.1947).

The banning of rickshaws and formal introduction of trishaws benefited the general populace. Competition between rickshaws and trishaws was intense. During this transitional stage, it was claimed that people chose to ride trishaws rather than the rickshaws (NAS, A000132/05, reel 3).

People began to think of rickshaw pullers as second-class labourers (NAS, A002034/13, reel 2). Trishaws could also fetch people and goods and did so speedily. The *Sin Chew Jit Poh* wrote that by 30 April 1947, people were shunning rickshaws to such an extent that only a few were still plying the roads, leaving 3,750 ex-pullers cooling their heels, pondering over their future. The reporter sympathetically interviewed a 67-year-old ex-puller on his way home to China, his dreams of massing a fortune for himself forever dashed. The journalist, however, believed that the trishaw industry was here to stay and would prosper (*Sin Chew Jit Poh*, 01.05.1947). *The Straits Times* also ran a personal feature article about the misfortune faced by a puller named Ah Tee, who picked up two school children only to be forced to transfer them to a trishaw by officials from the VRD, and then to have his rickshaw's licence plate confiscated. *The Straits Times* article ended ironically, stating, 'what does a licence plate matter anyway, he was probably thinking, as long as you still have the rickshaw?' (*The Straits Times*, 02.05.1947)

The abolition of the rickshaws brought mixed fortunes for the ex-pullers. It meant that men such as Ah Tee either faced repatriation to China or found other jobs to do. Knowing that the livelihood of these ex-rickshaw pullers would be adversely affected, the Municipal Commission sought to help them seek new employment. Jumabhoy felt that 'there was no problem for the government at that time for the employment of these people, except for very old people' (NAS, Transcript of A000074/37:94). Some became hawkers, while others decided to take up 'the humble occupations in the alleys and corners of Chinatown' (*The Straits Times*, 03.05.1947). Many ex-pullers logically switched to the more lucrative trishaw riding to survive but the older ex-rickshaw pullers were forcefully repatriated to China.

Repatriation of ex-rickshaw pullers

Several hundred rickshaw pullers could not switch to trishaw riding due to old age or ill-health and were repatriated to China. The ship carrying them set sail from Singapore and dropped them off at either Xiamen or Shantou. It was the same route taken decades earlier when they first migrated to Singapore, having embarked from the ports of Xiamen or Shantou in search of a better life. The repatriation scheme was shared by three government departments. The Labour Department would select those who would be sent back, the Immigration Department would provide the passage tickets, and the Social Welfare Department (SWD) would provide temporary housing

THE ADVENT OF THE TRISHAWS

for them at the Bushey Park and Borneo Depots before accompanying them to the ship. It was even possible that the ex-pullers could be repatriated without the knowledge of the Deputy Commissioner for Labour (NAS, ML 1919, LM 267/46, 19.03.1947). The ex-pullers were vaccinated and had their papers checked before they boarded the ship (NAS, ML 1919, LM 267/46, 11.03.1947). The future welfare of these 'destitute rickshaw pullers' (NAS, ML 1919, LM 267/46, 11.03.1947), however, was of no concern to the colonial government once they alighted at Xiamen or Shantou. Many of these ex-rickshawmen came from either Fuzhou (Foochow) or Xinghua (Henghua) prefectures in Fujian province, places nowhere near the ports of either Xiamen or Shantou. How they found their way home finally was of no concern to the Singapore authorities.

The Singapore Rickshaw and Trishaw Workers Union (SRTWU) also played a role in the repatriation scheme. On 19 December 1946, the SRTWU asked the Controller of Labour for assistance in offering alternative employment to ex-rickshaw pullers who were still fit for work and to repatriate those who were old and unable to work (NAS, ML 1919, LM 267/46, 19.12.1946). As a consequence, the Controller of Labour wrote to the Colonial Secretary for the approval of repatriating rickshaw pullers who could not do other work (NAS, ML 1919, LM 267/46, 30.12.1946). The Controller of Labour also noted an estimate made by the Customs Department that at least 90 per cent of the old rickshaw pullers were opium smokers. As they were 'unaccustomed to other form [sic] of labour', the Controller of Labour believed that 'it would be of benefit to Singapore if they were repatriated'. He noted that the cost of a ticket to Xiamen from Singapore was $110, and a further $10 would be required for each puller repatriated to get to his village from Xiamen. How he came to make these estimates was not explained, but he also noted that between 750 and 1,500 rickshaw pullers might be repatriated (NAS, ML 1919, LM 267/46, 30.12.1946).

On 15 February 1947, the Acting Commissioner for Labour, RH Oakeley, wrote a short memorandum to the Controller of Labour, informing him that the Colonial Secretary had agreed to pay for the cost of repatriating decrepit rickshaw pullers (NAS, ML 1919, LM 267/46, 15.02.1947). Following that, Oakeley wrote to the Secretary for Social Welfare to seek confirmation that the SWD could help obtain any certificates of vaccination of these pullers that could be required by the Immigration Officers. The Secretary for Social Welfare replied that his department could co-operate with the Labour Department in obtaining any certificates (NAS, ML 1919, LM 267/46, 18.02.1947 & 25.02.1947). Once the repatriation scheme was set in motion, the SRTWU premises at Bencoolen Street became packed to overflowing with personal belongings of repatriated ex-pullers, who had their names struck off the union register upon leaving Singapore. Initially the union was held responsible for vaccination of ex-pullers before the mistake was finally realised and responsibility transferred to the SWD (NAS, ML 1919, LM 267/46, undated). The union also gave ex-pullers a sum of money before their departure. The 56 who boarded the 'Hong Siang' and left on 7 April 1947, for instance, were given $2 each or the equivalent of several days' wages. Similarly, the 19 ex-pullers who left Singapore on board the 'Prosper' were also given $2 each (NAS, ML 1919, LM 267/46, 11.04.1947).

Dialect Group	Number Repatriated
Henghua	110
Hokchia	78
Hokkien (Minnanren)	37
Teochew	32
Foochow	4
Hakka (Kheh)	1
Dialect Group Not Available	17
Total	279

Table 1: Dialect group breakdown of repatriated ex-rickshaw pullers
Source: Figures compiled from 26 lists taken from NAS, LM 267/46.

Age Group	Number Repatriated
Below 40	5
Between 41 and 45	14
Between 46 and 50	44
Between 51 and 55	54
Between 56 and 60	60
Between 61 and 65	40
Between 66 and 70	13
Above 70	6
Age Not Available	43
Total	279

Table 2: Breakdown by age group of repatriated ex-rickshaw pullers
Source: Figures compiled from 26 lists taken from NAS, LM 267/46.

THE ADVENT OF THE TRISHAWS

All together, 400 ex-rickshawmen applied to the Labour Department to be repatriated. Of these applicants, 338 were approved and 320 actually repatriated (NAS, ML 1919, LM 267/46, 07.08.1947). The scheme lasted from February to August 1947 before the Deputy Commissioner for Labour put an end to it (NAS, ML 1919, LM 267/46, 05.07.1947). The names of 279 ex-rickshaw pullers who were repatriated under the auspices of the scheme were recorded and the breakdown of these ex-pullers by dialect group and age are shown in Tables 1 and 2. Most of those repatriated were either Henghua or Hokchia (188), and were aged between 51 and 60 (114 in all). However, this did not prevent the Henghua and Hokchia communities from monopolising the new trishaw industry.

Design, manufacture and inspection of trishaws

A trishaw consists of a bicycle and a sidecar, or a 'wooden bin' as one manufacturer put it (Ong Chwee Lan, interview, 14.07.1995).[4] Like many other types of trishaws in Southeast Asia, the trishaws in Singapore were made of locally available materials and parts – standard bicycle frames and wood (Meier 1977:56–63; Thomas 1981:37–44). Many assemblers were bicycle shop owners, which meant that trishaw renting and assembling were often a monopoly of bicycle shop owners. The trishaw industry came about in part because of the presence of a large number of bicycle repair shops during the Japanese Occupation. Chan Kwee Sung remembered many of these shops in Chinatown during that time and Low Ngiong Ing wrote that the Japanese also 'had a liking' for bicycles (Chan Kwee Sung, interview, 20.07.1995; Low 1973:6). Since there were no standard measurements, various types of trishaws appeared on the streets. Chan also remembered that the early trishaws during the Japanese Occupation had a bicycle fastened between the shafts of the rickshaw and then pedalled. However, the sight of the back of the trishaw rider drenched with perspiration was an 'uninviting sight'. Another model with the trishaw rider behind his passengers was not popular as 'passengers would feel their privacy invaded by his eyes behind' (Chan 2005:81–82).

---

[4] The interview with Madam Ong Chwee Lan, bicycle shop owner, was conducted in Hock Sin Hin Chop at 422 Joo Chiat Road. This shop was founded by the late Mr Ong Tuck Kin in 1949. Madam Ong, his daughter, took over the management of the shop in 1972.

The trishaws were manufactured locally in bicycle shops run by families. Locally available materials and parts are mostly used along with standard bicycle frames and a wooden trishaw base. The trishaw has to be designed, manufactured and maintained efficiently, for it is meant to carry loads of up to 175 kilogrammes for distances of up to several kilometres. In countries such as India, the design of trishaws varied from region to region, with those from Bengal considered the worst (Thomas 1981:40–43). In Singapore, the Municipal Commission moved to standardise the measurements of the trishaw frame in 1946 and again in 1948 (CSGGS, S277, 21.12.1946; CSGGS, S36, 08.12.1948). The dimensions of the Singapore trishaw were as follows:

Wheel base	4' (about 1 m 22 cm)
Height from top of hood to ground	4'8" (about 1 m 42 cm)
Width of body	2'6" (about 76 cm)
Length of body	4'2" (about 1 m 27 cm)
Overall width of trishaw	4'2" (about 1 m 27 cm)
Overall length of trishaw	6'4" (about 1 m 93 cm)

Table 3: Dimensions of the trishaw in Singapore in 1948
Source: The Trisha (Regulation and Licensing) Regulations, No. S.277, 21 December 1946, and the Municipal (Trisha) By-Laws, No. S.36, 8 December 1948.

The standardised dimensions of the trishaw remained the same for both years except that its height from the top of the hood to the ground was increased from 4 ft 2 inches (about 1 m 27 cm) in 1946 to 4 ft 8 inches (about 1 m 42 cm) in 1948. Furthermore, each trishaw was taxed $12 every six months.

Like many Chinese enterprises, the bicycle shop was generally a family run business (*The New Nation*, 29.04.1980). With the average number of people working in a shop, including an apprentice or two, it often took about three days to a week for a trishaw to be assembled. The necessary parts had to be made available first. The bicycle shop owners, who would often become trishaw owners in the end, imported bicycles primarily from China. They would purchase the metal parts from other bicycle shops and wooden parts from carpenters. The wooden framework for the customised sidecar (built according to the measurements in Table 3) would be nailed together first and then covered with aluminium. The collapsible metal frame that supported the cover would be fitted. A metal frame was then welded to the bicycle –

THE ADVENT OF THE TRISHAWS

with two axles under the handlebars and a third one at the centre of the back wheel. A bicycle was then bolted to the sidecar and a third wheel attached to the left side of the sidecar.

A ride in a trishaw was meant to be comfortable for the public. For this reason, the seat was tilted slightly backwards. The wooden base of the sidecar was also positioned at an angle. The seat was cushioned and an overhead shade attached to the sidecar by means of the adjustable metal frame. Another hood or flap at the front kept the sidecar totally closed when it rained, leaving only the cyclist unprotected. The early trishaws were painted many colours; some even had cartoons depicted on them. However, because many children were inevitably attracted to the trishaws by the cartoons, accidents did occur. As a result, the Labour Front (LF) government under Lim Yew Hock as Chief Minister ordered that all trishaws simply be painted green (NAS, A000669/16, reel 13; Nanyang Daxue Lishi Xi 1971:50).[5] By the 1980s, trishaw-making was a dying trade and a trishaw maker would build between 10 and 15 trishaws per month, depending on the demand (*The New Nation*, 29.04.1980).

Government regulation also made it explicitly clear that a trishaw could only carry either two adults, or an adult and a child under three feet in height, or three children under three feet in height (CSGGS, S277, 21.12.1946; CSGGS, S36, 08.12.1948). The seat was comfortable and rather low; children would have no problem boarding and alighting. Since the trishaw had no gears, the rider had to always exert the same amount of pressure and energy on the pedals to keep the trishaw going. His only means of warning oncoming traffic was his bell and the brakes. The former was, however, usually not loud enough to be heard by oncoming cars and this forced trishaw riders to keep their vehicle on the extreme edge of the left lane of the main thoroughfares. The brakes were powerful enough to stop the entire vehicle at short notice.

Periodic trishaw inspections by the VRD were usually preceded by intense activity to ensure that the trishaw would pass the test. The entire trishaw could be lost if it failed inspection. Hence, before the inspection, the trishaw was brought to the bicycle shop by the cyclist where it was cleaned and repaired thoroughly. Torn seats and hoods were replaced. The chain and sprocket of the wheels would be oiled so that the trishaw would travel smoothly. The brakes were also tested; if they were deemed defective by the

---

[5] Unfortunately, the authors failed to say when the law was promulgated, and who first proposed it.

shop workers, a new set would be attached. Most inspectors emphasised the safety aspect of the brakes, not surprising with the increasingly heavier traffic on the roads as the years went by. During the inspection, the inspector was often taken for a short ride by the rider and the verdict only issued upon the inspector's return to the VRD.

There was no fixed price for a trishaw and many riders actually owned their own vehicle. Tan Ai Mai bought his trishaw for $80 in 1947. He also remembered many riders buying their trishaws from 'trishaw shops' (NAS, A000132/05, reel 3). A brand new one could cost between $500 and $600 in the 1950s, although the prices varied according to the bicycle shop manufacturers. Madam Ong Chwee Lan even remembered trishaw prices as between $800 and $900 at one stage. Since the trishaw manufacturers were often trishaw owners at the same time, many bicycle shops owned fleets of trishaws which were rented out to prospective riders. Under such circumstances, rather than rent, it was better to buy a second-hand trishaw from another rider who gave the job up. That was how Lu Tian Lee purchased his first vehicle for only $100. He then bought a brand new one in 1947 for $350 when he got rid of his second-hand trishaw.

Another trishaw rider, Ng Kah Eng, bought a second-hand trishaw for $300 in 1947 and rode that until he became a full-time staff member of the SHTRA in 1961. Lim Hong Cher bought his trishaw for 'more than $200' in 1956 (NAS, A000745/06, reel 6). A trishaw rider who wanted to be known only as 'Ah Tong' bought his sturdy second-hand trishaw for $200 in the late 1960s – a telling sign that the value and role of the trishaw was already beginning to decline less than two decades after rickshaws were abolished in Singapore (NAS, A000669/16, reel 11; NAS, Transcript of A000117/09:46; 'Ah Tong', interview, 12.07.1995). By 1980, a brand new trishaw could be sold for $550 (*The New Nation*, 29.04.1980).

The trishaw as a key mode of transport

The re-introduction of trishaws in Singapore in mid-1942 was in response to the general need, under wartime conditions, to provide the public with a cheap, convenient and efficient means of transport. The scarcity of petrol and the large numbers of bicycles brought to the island under the Japanese Military Administration led to the birth of the trishaw. It was easy to build, required few labourers and could be sold or rented out for a decent sum of money. The trishaw also travelled faster than the rickshaw and the presence

THE ADVENT OF THE TRISHAWS

of this new and innovative means of public transport also caught the attention of the Japanese administrators and military. If they did not have a motorcar (or if they could not requisition one for themselves), they could travel around the island on a trishaw. This was a new experience for both the trishaw riders and the passengers, even if the riders remained fearful of picking up Japanese soldiers.

While the Japanese welcomed the presence of trishaws in Singapore to help ease traffic woes on the island, the new mode of transport was regarded as a social problem for the returning British colonial authorities in 1945. Initially the BMA had to deal with the administrative problems that came with the end of the war and the seizure of all Japanese assets as 'enemy property'. Since the trishaws were leased by Japanese firms, the vehicles were seized as well. It took some time for the British to realise that there was no way the riders could produce evidence of any wartime transactions they had made with the Japanese. In addition, there were alleged malpractices by trishaw owners and problems relating to trishaw licences and fees that had their origins in the Japanese Occupation.

By 1946, the British had realised that it would take some time for public transport to be restored. Trishaws were needed once again to provide the means of transport demanded by the general public. What the British did that was different from the Japanese Military Administration was to monitor and regulate the nascent trishaw industry before it became too difficult to control. Therefore, by 1948, with so many trishaws plying the streets, the colonial authorities felt the need to regulate the number of trishaws and standardise the dimensions of the vehicle. This marked an early start of government regulation of the trishaw industry.

The continued presence of the trishaws did not bode well for the rickshaw pullers. Those pullers who were younger and strong enough could make the switch to trishaw riding. Elderly rickshaw pullers who were too old or weak to make the transition were repatriated to China and their dreams of earning a substantial amount of money were forever shattered. The ban of the rickshaws on humanitarian grounds in 1947 increased the public's dependence on the trishaws as a mode of transport. Bicycle shops began manufacturing trishaws to be sold or rented out to the riders. Periodic inspections of trishaws had to be carried out by the VRD to ensure that the trishaws were safe enough to ply the streets. The large numbers of trishaws gave the riders some measure of political clout, an issue that will be examined in the next chapter.

Chapter 3

THE TRISHAW INDUSTRY AS A '*BANG*'-BASED TRADE[1]

The *bang* structure of Singapore Chinese society

The Chinese in Singapore have never been a single ethnic community. Due to their demographic dominance, the Chinese had 'recreate[d] a Chinese community outside the original homeland, but with more appealing political and economic conditions' (Safran 1991:89). In practice, however, the Singapore Chinese were divided into dialect groups, each of which constituted a *bang*. According to Cheng, the '*bang*' is a very old social concept and in Singapore came to signify 'a Chinese politico-socio-economic grouping based principally on a dialect' (Cheng 1985:23). Nearly all Chinese born in Singapore can trace their ancestry to prefectures, townships and villages in the two south-eastern provinces of Fujian and Guangdong. There are five major dialect groups in Singapore – the Hokkiens, Teochews, Cantonese, Hakka (or Kheh) and Hainanese (in order of economic dominance). There are also four smaller dialect groups – the Foochows, Henghuas, Hokchias and 'Sanjiangren' (a local term of convenience which lumped together all Chinese born outside Fujian and Guangdong provinces).

The Singapore Chinese congregated in different groups because of the helplessness experienced as individual Chinese settlers, and the need to defend themselves during emergencies (Suyama 1962:198). Following the British encouragement of mass migration to Malaya and Singapore to work in the rubber plantations and the tin mines especially, even more Chinese left

---

[1] An earlier version of this chapter was published in *Journal of the Malaysian Branch of the Royal Asiatic Society*, 69 (2), December 1996.

THE TRISHAW INDUSTRY AS A *'BANG'*-BASED TRADE

Southeast China in search of a better livelihood. By the 1920s these numbers had reached the scale of a great exodus. For instance, during the Northern Expedition led by Chiang Kai-shek against the warlords in 1926–1927, a total of 707,855 Chinese entered Singapore alone (Cui 1994:18–20; Ee 1961:33–39). The Chinese population in Singapore peaked at about 418,600 in the last official census of 1931 prior to the Japanese Occupation (Chiew 1995:43).

However, this mass migration of Chinese to Singapore was never seen by new migrants to necessarily be permanent. Crissman noted that:

> Leaving a home was not thought to be permanent but, on the contrary, was seen as a temporary expedient that would allow them to earn enough to live, support their families, and eventually return home as wealthy men (Crissman 1967:187).

Consequently, the Singapore Chinese society became 'segmented' as each dialect group formed a *bang*, out of necessity to protect their communal interests. Upon settling in a foreign place like Singapore with so many Chinese speaking different dialects, migrants would organise and usually form a group on the basis of lineage, clan, dialect, home village, township, prefecture, province and occupation (Cheng 1985:28). Mak rightly asserts that 'a dialect is only an expression of a subculture related to it' and that 'it is not the dialect but the related subculture that generates the group identity' (Mak 1995:2).

One way that a *bang* could come together was to found associations, clans and guilds to serve its fellow members. These associations would provide shelter, food, clothing, jobs and other basic social welfare needs of members (Carstens 1975; Cheng 1990:57–71; Cheng 1995:67–77; Hsieh 1978:184–226; Tan 1986:68–84; Yan 1991:59–64; Yao 1984:75–88). It is important to note, however, that certain trades and occupations in Singapore were monopolised by particular dialect groups. This was because earlier migrants who entered Singapore chose particular occupations along dialect lines. Since they spoke the same language, by working and living together they eventually established, by virtue of capital and numbers, dominance over particular occupations. Later migrants from the same dialect group were often introduced into that occupation to ensure a continued stranglehold on it by that group. Therefore, what eventually happened in Singapore over the decades was that nearly every newly arrived Chinese got 'compartmentalised' in terms of possible employment prospects. Through a process of 'involution, exclusion, competition, regression and succession', an economic niche for a particular dialect group was carved out (Cheng 1985:89). The guilds, in particular, were founded to control the supply and flow of materials and information pertaining to particular trades, to prevent people outside the guild (that is, from other dialect groups) from entering the trade (Mak 1995:77).

These marked divisions into *bang* did not mean, however, that any dialect group could necessarily completely monopolise a particular trade or occupational specialisation. For instance, the Hainanese used to dominate the coffee shop business but surrendered control to the Foochows after World War II. Generally, however, a person from one dialect group could not find work easily in an occupation regulated by another dialect group. Thus, a *bang* established in a more recent period, such as those of the Henghuas and Hokchias, could not penetrate job markets dominated by other *bangs* that had preceded them. However, the Henghuas and Hokchias proved to be no exception to the rule when it came to organising themselves by *bangs* in the early part of the twentieth century.

The Henghuas of Singapore

The Henghuas come from Xinghua Prefecture in northern Fujian province. The prefecture itself consisted of two districts – Putian and Xianyou – with Henghuas from the latter district arriving first to work in the tin mines of Malaya in the second half of the nineteenth century. The Henghuas arrived in Singapore much later than the Hokkiens, the dominant *bang* in Singapore. Yan remarked sardonically that 'when the Henghuas finally settled down here [in Singapore], the Hokkiens were already millionaires' (Yan 1972:34). The Henghuas constitute one of the minority dialect groups in Singapore; in 1947, only 1 per cent of the Chinese were Henghuas. Of the 7,446 Henghuas, almost 90 per cent of them lived in the city area at the time (Del Tufo 1949:294–295). The Henghuas first entered Singapore from the late nineteenth century. By that time, most ordinary jobs that one could do were already monopolised by some other dialect group. Even the collection of human faeces from public toilets for farmers, a job considered to be demeaning or worse, had just been taken up by Teochews and Henghuas could make no inroads into the occupation. However, with the import into Singapore of rickshaws from Japan through Shanghai in 1880, the Henghuas entered the nascent rickshaw industry, giving them the ideal opportunity they needed to create their own *bang* (NAS, A000132/05, reel 3). The other dialect groups had a bad impression of rickshaw pulling and were involved in trades of their own, and hence considered rickshaw pulling demeaning work (Yan 1972:34).

When a new Henghua migrant arrived in Singapore, he would only feel safe in the company of fellow Henghuas.[2] The old-timers would then help the greenhorns find a job, but the only occupation available would invariably be one monopolised by the Henghuas who migrated earlier – rickshaw pulling. The *bang* structure and social stratification of occupation made it explicitly clear that rickshaw pulling was a job designated primarily for Henghuas. Following improvements in public transport from the first half of the early twentieth century, the Henghuas diversified interests into the bicycle, taxi, bus, trishaw and later on, automobile spare parts industries.

There is a link between the role of the Henghuas in the bicycle industry and the rise and demise of the trishaw. The first Chinese to venture into the bicycle trade was a Henghua named Yeow Kee (Nanyang Daxue Lishi Xi 1971:34–35). He established the Hock Leong Hin Bicycle Company in Kuala Lumpur which, with careful organisation, prospered. He employed many workers and apprentices who, after gaining experience for themselves under him, left the company and migrated to other parts of Malaya as well as Indonesia to set up their own bicycle shops. From the turn of the century on, the number of Henghuas involved in the bicycle trade increased, which led to their dominance of the trade in Singapore.

Initially, the Henghuas were considered a part of the Fujian (i.e. Hokkien) *bang* but it was felt by the end of World War I that a Henghua association was needed to represent the growing Henghua community in Singapore after observing Chinese from other *bang* groups organising various clan and dialect associations. Therefore, in 1920, they left the Hokkien *bang* and organised the Hin Ann Huay Kuan. The Henghua community used to live in districts 7 and 8 on the outskirts of the city: Weld Road, Jalan Besar, Sungei Road, Rochor Road, Rochor Canal Road and Bencoolen Street (Cheng 1993:38).

The Hokchias of Singapore

The Hokchias – known as Hokcheng in the Hokkien dialect – also came from northern Fujian province. They hailed from Fuqing District in Fuzhou Prefecture. According to Cheng, there were Hokchia-speaking Hokchias and Henghua-speaking Hokchias, both regarding themselves as Hokchia,

---

[2] For an in-depth study of the origins and social organisation of the rickshaw industry in Singapore, see Warren (1986), especially Chapters 6 and 9.

which created confusion in the minds of outsiders (Cheng 1985:23). Like the Henghuas, the Hokchias came to Singapore relatively late when compared to the Hokkiens and major dialect groups. The Hokchias are also considered a minority dialect group. The same 1947 census cited earlier for the Henghuas recorded that only 0.9 per cent of Singapore Chinese were Hokchias. Out of 6,323 Hokchias in Singapore in 1947, about 93 per cent lived in the city area (Del Tufo 1949:294–295).

It was unclear which *bang* first started the rickshaw industry; but eventual control of the business would be shared by the Henghuas and Hokchias. Like the Henghuas, the Hokchias in China were a rural people, who could not put their agricultural skills to best use in Singapore. Consequently, when rickshaws were first introduced in 1880, the Hokchias also became involved in the industry. In 1947, following the ban on rickshaws in Singapore, the Hokchias came to dominate the new trishaw industry. By the early 1970s, the Hokchia-speaking Hokchias had moved on to working in the bus transport industry, leaving the Henghua-speaking Hokchias to continue in trishaw riding.

The Singapore Futsing Association (SFA) was established by Hokchias in 1910. Initially, it was meant to be a communal meeting place for the Hokchias but it later assumed responsibility for mutual aid and other welfare benefits on behalf of the Hokchias (SFA 1982:45 & 54). The early Hokchia migrants resided in the residential territory of the Hokkiens. With the increasing number of Hokchias settling in Singapore, they moved out of Hokkien-speaking areas and shared districts 7 and 8 with the Henghuas, although they confined themselves to Victoria Street, Johore Road, Ophir Road, Queen Street, Anguilla Road, Muar Road, Tiwary Street and Ban San Street (SFA 1982:80). However, between the two groups, the Hokchias were economically weaker.

The Hokchias too were heavily involved in the road transport industry. In Singapore, the Ongs from Jiangdou village in Xinghua Prefecture dominated the bicycle industry and the formation of the Singapore Kang Tou Ong Clansmen Association in 1974 reflected their skill in the industry (Cheng 1993:47). The late Ong Ban Koh was the first (Henghua-speaking) Hokchia to be involved in the bicycle industry. The industry was an example of how one *bang* relinquished control to another *bang*. The Hokkiens founded the bicycle industry when Ong and his partner Teo Sock Guan opened a shop along Victoria Street in 1909. Ong later left the partnership and opened his own shop in Hill Street. The Hokkiens gradually lost interest in the bicycle industry as they came to dominate other trades, particularly the lucrative rubber market and industry. Eventually, they relinquished the industry to the Hokchias and Henghuas (Nanyang Daxue Lishi Xi 1971:40–41).

Prior to the Japanese Occupation, the Henghuas and Hokchias, despite monopolising control of the transport industry, often clashed with each other, sometimes violently. The Henghua rickshaw pullers were considered by the British to be 'the most truculent group' of Chinese and disagreements over territorial boundaries often arose between pullers of both dialect groups. In 1938, large-scale fighting broke out over rickshaw rentals and the right to strike (Warren 1986:117–127). A decade later, in 1948, another violent conflict broke out but this time a representative of the Hokkien Huay Kuan met 20 leaders of the Henghua and Hokchia communities to settle the dispute by arbitration. As a result, the Singapore Hock Puah Sang Communities Union (now known as the Singapore Hockposian Association) was founded (Cheng 1993:47; SFA 1982:82; Peng 1983:L-38 & L-39). Under its auspices, both communities agreed to 'foster friendship and exchange knowledge between members' as well as promising 'to promote unity and public welfare' among themselves (Constitution of the Singapore Hockposian Association, Article 4, Chapter 1).

The Hui Ann Hokkiens in Singapore

A brief word must also be made about this particular group of trishaw riders. In addition to Henghuas and Hokchias, trishaw riding was also taken up by Hokkiens who came from Hui Ann District in Fujian province. However, only those Hui Ann Hokkiens who came from the northern part of the district spoke Henghua. The first Hui Ann Hokkiens settled in the Tanjong Pagar area in District 2 such as Duxton Road, Duxton Hill, Craig Road and Tras Street. Like the Henghuas and Hokchias, they also arrived far later than the dominant dialect groups, and hence they chose to either be stevedores, coal heavers or rickshaw pullers. Some Hui Ann Hokkiens later became tugboat owners and partially controlled trading on the Singapore River. The majority of them later gave up rickshaw pulling and entered the construction industry during the post-war boom (Ou 1991:77–78). The Duxton Road residents originated primarily from three clans: Ho, Teo and Chng. Feuding among all three clans was common before the war (Tanjong Pagar Citizens' Consultative Committee 1989:93). When that happened, the Hui Ann Association would act as their mediator (Oral History Department 1990:38). The Ho Clan used to own a large fleet of trishaws which they rented out on a daily basis to prospective riders. It seemed that only Hokkien trishaw riders would wear a blue jacket while riding the vehicle: the Henghuas and Hokchias eschewed any 'uniform' (NAS, A000280/20, reel 19).

The trishaw owners

In 1971, it was estimated that 80 per cent of trishaw owners were Henghuas, with the majority also involved in the repair and assembling of trishaws (Nanyang Daxue Lishi Xi 1971:51–52). It was clear too then that the trishaw industry was restricted to the Chinese and the *bang* structure ensured Henghua control over it. It is, therefore, not surprising that the Henghuas founded the STOA to represent their overall interests in the trade (Peng 1983:L-37; Wu 1975:110). The STOA was initially established during the Japanese Occupation but as the British were no longer the colonial masters, it was not registered under the Societies Ordinance of 1909 (NAS, MHA 445, R of S 181/47, 20.04.1946). The Societies Ordinance required compulsory registration of *all* societies but 'was not designed to encourage and promote the development of trade unions along sound lines' (Siddiqi 1967:7). The Societies Ordinance was augmented by the Trade Unions Ordinance of 1940 which came into effect on 1 July 1941. No union, however, was registered under the Trade Unions Ordinance before the Japanese Occupation. By 1941, there were 263 societies either registered or exempted from registration under the Societies Ordinance, most of them Chinese trade guilds (Gamba 1962:7).

Once the war ended, and the BMA relinquished their control over Malaya and Singapore, a new civilian government was established on 1 April 1946. Within a year, the Trade Union Adviser of Malaya – a government official appointed 'to assist and encourage the early development of the trade union movement in the Malayan Union on sound and well-proven lines' (Gamba 1962:103) – announced that all new societies and unions had to be registered within one month of founding. Until then, associations of 'whatever kind' could be organised (Purcell 1965:353). The Societies Ordinance for *all existing societies* in Singapore was brought back on the books in April 1947 and registration of *all existing unions* was to be carried out by the end of September 1946 (Cheng 1950:11; Stenson 1970:134). The STOA fell into the latter registration category and on 20 April 1946 asked the Registry of Societies (ROS) for the new registration forms to meet the dateline (NAS, MHA 445, R of S 181/47, 20.04.1946).

THE TRISHAW INDUSTRY AS A *'BANG'*-BASED TRADE

Who exactly were the post-war trishaw owners? While several major rickshaw owners became trishaw owners upon abolition of rickshaws in 1947, the original trishaw owners were largely a different group of rent-capitalists altogether. They were primarily proprietors of bicycle, tricycle and trishaw enterprises. There were 40 members in the STOA in April 1946, nearly all of them representing individual businesses. These transport enterprises were mostly spread across Chinatown,[3] Little India[4] and the inner city area, with five in Victoria Street and another five situated in Queen Street. Furthermore, it is quite significant that the STOA in 1946 was housed at 189, Waterloo Street, which was also the location of the Teck Huat Tricycle Company, whose proprietor Lim Teck Tong served as secretary of the STOA from 1949 to 1960! (NAS, MHA 445, R of S 181/47, 20.04.1946). A list of proposed office-bearers submitted to the ROS in December 1950 confirmed that out of 30 people named, 18 were 'bicycle dealers' while another seven were 'trishaw dealers' (NAS, MHA 445, R of S 181/47, 20.12.1950).

The STOA was officially registered on 5 February 1947 and, right from the start, it was beset with problems. In September 1949, a rival organisation, the Trishaw Industry Proprietors and Manufacturers Association of Singapore (TIPMAS) was registered and located itself at 84-A Bencoolen Street with an initial membership of thirty (SSAR 1949:94). Originally, the Rickshaw Owners Association had re-applied for registration under the Trade Unions Ordinance on 28 May 1949 but it eventually registered itself as TIPMAS on 27 June. The new organisation was open to all *Chinese* who owned more than five trishaws.[5] Even before TIPMAS was registered, the STOA knew that it would be registered and the latter warned that this 'might spoilt (sic) the good works of the STOA'. The STOA saw its soon-to-be registered rival as 'ample proof that some persons will cause unrest'

---

[3] Chinatown refers to three areas within the inner city area. Kreta Ayer is the area bounded by Upper Cross Street, New Bridge Road, South Bridge Road, Neil Road and Kreta Ayer Road. Telok Ayer the area south of it up to Cecil Street. And Bukit Pasoh is the area west of Kreta Ayer up to Cantonment Road. These areas lie in Districts 1 and 2.

[4] Little India is the area in District 8 bounded by Syed Alwi Road, Sungei Road, Serangoon Road and Jalan Besar.

[5] The Registry of Societies claimed that TIPMAS could not be traced in their records in a letter (reference ROS 9/66) addressed to me on 26 April 1995. Some of the records of TIPMAS are, however, located at NAS but permission must be sought from the Registry of Trade Unions (RTU). Unfortunately, the author does not have access to all its records. An RTU official informed him that some of these records, although more than 50 years old, are still 'confidential' and therefore remain closed.

for the STOA. Lim Teck Tong, the then secretary of the STOA, wrote to the ROS declaring that 'in every civilised country and nation there are *no two organisations of the same nature*' (NAS, MHA 445, R of S 181/47, 21.03.1949).[6]

TIPMAS, however, was in no position to challenge the STOA for control of the industry. In 1949, TIPMAS had 30 members; the STOA had 285. In 1950, TIPMAS increased its membership to 64, but the STOA had risen to 360 members! And although there were 78 members in TIPMAS by 1951, the association suddenly dissolved itself after discovering that its certificate of registration had been 'obtained by mistake'. In September 1950, the Registrar of Trade Unions had discovered that some members of TIPMAS were not actually employers of trishaw riders, but merely hired the trishaws out for rent to interested trishaw riders. Consequently, TIPMAS was not considered by the Registrar to be a trade union within the perimeters set by the Trade Unions Ordinance, and the association was asked to 'voluntarily dissolve' itself (NAS, ML 922, RTU 190, 27.11.1950). The decision to dissolve itself was made at an Annual General Meeting of the association on 30 September 1951. The certificate of registration was withdrawn by the Registry of Trade Unions (RTU) on 6 November (NAS, ML 922, RTU 190, 09.11.1951 & 16.11.1951).

In any case, the STOA also voluntarily disbanded in the same year, after the Registrar of Trade Unions found that it too had not met all the demands laid down by the Trade Unions Ordinance of 1940 (SSAR 1949:99–100; SSAR 1950:80–81; SSAR 1951:85–86). This could have been a source of frustration for the STOA. On 5 December 1946, the secretary of the association, Lim Teck Tong, had written to the Registrar of Trade Unions, asking him if the STOA was to register under the Trade Unions Ordinance or the Societies Ordinance. The Registrar replied that the Trade Union Adviser was drafting the rules for the STOA to fit the Trade Unions Ordinance. Lim was instructed to complete an application form for registration 'as a Trade Union on the move' (NAS, ML 922, RTU 190, 05.12.1946 & 14.12.1946). Yet the RTU was to find that the STOA did not meet the demands of the Trade Unions Ordinance almost five years later! The STOA dissolved itself at an Annual General Meeting on 30 June 1951, and the association was officially de-registered on 10 July. Lim also wrote to the Registrar of Trade Unions that all the assets of the association would be transferred to the new STOA that would be registered under the Societies Ordinance (NAS, ML

---

[6] Emphasis added.

THE TRISHAW INDUSTRY AS A '*BANG*'-BASED TRADE

922, RTU 190, 02.07.1951). The new STOA had been officially re-registered as a society on 11 April 1951.

It is not known how many trishaws on average each member of the STOA owned. According to rule 4(a) of the STOA Rules and Regulations, occupation membership was open to all people who owned at least one trishaw as well as to other individuals who had connections with the trishaw industry. Initially, in 1949, the STOA looked after the interests and welfare of both the trishaw owners and the riders who owned their own vehicles (NAS, MHA 445, R of S 181/47, 21.03.1950). But in the following year, the riders founded the SHTRA, leaving the STOA a purely owners' association. There are no records extant which show that a trishaw rider could eventually have enough capital and work his way up to become a trishaw owner. Undoubtedly, this did occur as Warren has demonstrated the same pattern of upward social mobility for rickshaw pullers in a somewhat more difficult economic climate and circumstance in pre-war Singapore (Warren 1986). The trishaws were manufactured and then either sold or rented out by the manufacturers and owners from their bicycle, tricycle or trishaw shops. However, there are cases where a trishaw rider managed to own more than one trishaw and thus rent out his 'spare' vehicle to someone else. Koh Teong Koo, for instance, initially bought a trishaw for himself. However, following the Japanese surrender, he returned to Singapore from China and then bought five trishaws at $200 each in order to cash in on the post-war recovery. He rode his own trishaw and rented the others to fellow riders. He later sold all five vehicles when he moved on to the Cameron Highlands (NAS, A000136/06, reel 6). However, he joined the SHTRA instead of the STOA, which implied that he never really saw himself as an 'owner'.

Trishaws were rented out daily to prospective riders regardless of dialect group or nationality. A deposit of about $100 was usually required for loan of the vehicle prior to 1948. After 1948, when identity cards were introduced as part of the Malayan Emergency regulations, deposits were no longer required (NAS, transcript of A000117/09:52). Ong Tuck Kin, the proprietor of Hock Sin Hin Chop at 422 Joo Chiat Road in eastern Singapore, owned as many as 200 trishaws and rented them out to anybody who wanted to use them. All he did was to record the prospective rider's name and the trishaw was rented out for $1 per day. Most riders were 'part-timers' who did odd jobs such as rubbish collecting during the early morning, and rode trishaws to pick up tourists in the afternoons. Some of these riders often took Ong's trishaws and then sublet them out to other individuals (Ong Chwee Lan, interview, 14.07.1995). Rent was ordinarily fixed at $1 per day at Hock Sin Hin Chop, one of the larger trishaw agencies; on Sundays, no rent was demanded by the proprietor. However, different owners charged different rates in different eras. Lu Tian Lee rented his trishaw for $4 per day in 1946. In the same year, Tan Low Kee paid as much as $6 per day for his trishaw. Trishaw riders worked in two shifts: one from 5 am to 2 pm and the other for the rest of the day (Ong Chwee Lan, interview, 14.07.1995; NAS, A000669/16, reel 11; NAS, A000895/06, reel 5). Tan Ai Mai remembered paying $1 rent per day but the rent was dependent on the condition of the trishaw on lease (NAS, A000132/05, reel 3). On certain public occasions, rents would not be collected at all. One of the most important of them was the charity ride in April 1954 to raise funds for Nanyang University, the first Chinese-language university in Southeast Asia. After a meeting with Chng Keng Swee, President of the SHTRA, the STOA decided not to collect rent for trishaw riders participating in the fund-raising drive (Ou 1992:5; Nanyang Daxue 1956:370).

Trishaw owners were expected to bear most of the costs of damage incurred to their vehicles. From registering to repairing and maintaining a trishaw, the owner had to pay for all expenses, except tyre repairs. Lu Tian Lee noted sarcastically that all the owners ever cared about were the rents they collected. Since owners had to bear the costs for damages and loss, many of them refused to repair a trishaw if the damage was minor. An ignorant rider would then rent the flawed vehicle, and if the trishaw broke down, it was the gullible rider who had to push it to the nearest bicycle shop, get it fixed, and only be reimbursed by the owner when he sent it back (NAS, A000669/16, reel 11).

On the other hand, the owners argued that the riders should not complain as it was the former who had to bear virtually all the maintenance costs. Madam Ong Chwee Lan noted that all a rider had to do was to bring the broken-down trishaw back and it would be fixed. However, the rider would not be given another trishaw – he simply had to wait until 'his' trishaw was repaired. Madam Ong also observed that the Joo Chiat area where Hock Sin Hin Chop was located had many trishaw enterprises. The impatient or destitute rider could easily approach a nearby enterprise and rent another trishaw to work (Ong Chwee Lan, interview, 14.07.1995). Furthermore, free compressed air was available outside every bicycle shop if a trishaw tyre went flat, and the mending of a punctured tube cost only five cents (Chia 1984:80–81)!

The STOA, originally founded to protect the interests of the trishaw owners, did not have a good working relationship with the ROS. Time and again, from its inception in 1947 up to its eventual closure in 1978, the ROS demanded that the STOA amend its rules. Some amendments were required as the STOA originally submitted very vague rules about the structure and organisation of the association. Often, however, the ROS wanted the rules to be re-phrased to make them more readily accessible and intelligible to all parties concerned. For instance, three months before its second registration in April 1951, the ROS insisted the STOA change rule 41 ('These rules shall become effective after they have been passed at the General Meeting of Members and approved by the Registrar of Societies') to read: 'These rules shall become effective after they have been passed at the General Meeting of Members and approved by the Registrar of Societies *in writing*' (NAS, R of S 181/47, 16.01.1951).[7] Every time a legal mistake was discovered, or an amendment required, the STOA had to submit two fresh carbon copies of its rules and regulations in English and Mandarin for approval by the ROS. This had to be observed as it would otherwise be 'illegal for any person to organise or take part in any activity of or on behalf of the Association' (NAS, MHA 445, R of S 181/47, 25.01.1951).

Furthermore the STOA, as a registered society, was obliged to submit its annual returns and list of office-bearers to the ROS every year; the ROS then checked with the Criminal Investigation Department (CID) concerning the possible criminal records of office-bearers. Tan Lean was appointed as Chinese Clerk by the STOA in early 1965, and the ROS immediately checked with the CID for any criminal links. The CID replied that Tan was summoned on 12 October 1953 and 13 August 1954 for failing to keep proper account books and had been fined $20 and $10 respectively (NAS, MHA 445, R of S 181/47, 22.02.1965). After a meeting with the secretary of the STOA on 2 April 1965, the ROS ordered the STOA to replace Tan and submit particulars of his replacement (NAS, MHA 445, R of S 181/47, 02.04.1965). Tan vigorously protested his innocence with respect to the second charge and was granted an interview by the Registrar of Societies but he never took up the STOA appointment. Instead, it went to Lee King Tiong, who apparently had no criminal record (NAS, MHA 445, R of S 181/47, 06.04.1965, 13.04.1965 & 12.05.1965).

The trishaw riders

In 1947, the year rickshaws were abolished, there were 730,133 Chinese in Singapore and 38 per cent of them were born in China (Del Tufo 1949:327).

---

[7] Emphasis added.

A SLOW RIDE INTO THE PAST

They had fled their villages, migrated to Singapore and began a new life as rickshaw pullers. Tay Quay Muay, born in Fuqing in 1906, was forced to abandon his village in 1927 when bandits overran the area. Upon arrival in Singapore, fellow Hokchias introduced him to rickshaw pulling. In 1930, however, he gave it up and worked first in a rubber factory and then as a farmer in Johore. In 1945, when the Japanese surrendered, he returned to Singapore and took up trishaw riding since 'it made good money' (NAS, Transcript of A000739/03:1–20). Similarly, Lu Tian Lee left his village in Hui Ann District in 1935 because of political instability and social unrest in the region, despite his father's protests against leaving China. In the end, though, his father reluctantly paid his $18 fare and Lu left Xiamen, only returning to China years later for his marriage. After his marriage and despite his father's objection again, Lu returned to Singapore (NAS, A000669/16, reel 4).

Many trishaw riders had little education and, at a time when Hokkien was the lingua franca of the Singapore Chinese community, few could speak Mandarin.[8] Ng Kar Eng, treasurer of the SHTRA from 1961 to 1983, recalled that most of its members received a few years of classical education in China but they could not speak Mandarin. In a survey of 40 trishaw riders in Singapore in 1961, it was found that 'the group as a whole has very little or no education' – only one rider completed Primary Six in a Chinese school (Wee 1962:28–29). Therefore, meetings of the SHTRA were conducted in Hokkien even though some trishaw riders did not fully understand the language. In the context of cultural bilingualism, as the association was dominated by Henghuas and Hokchias, dialect groups who spoke mutually unintelligible languages, it was considered absolutely necessary for a Henghua and Hokchia committee member to be present at the association's premises (NAS, Transcript of A000117/09:84–89).

Trishaw riders mainly resided in areas traditionally linked to the Henghuas and Hokchias – that is, districts 7 and 8. According to a rare two-volume membership subscription book compiled between 1971 and 1976, there were 228 members of the SHTRA listed. That list of 228 names showed that between 1971 and 1976, trishaw riders had moved their residence northwards away from the old rickshaw lodgings of the pre-war

---

[8] This was still evident when I first did my fieldwork in mid-1995. The trishaw riders I attempted to interview spoke only Hokkien. Even when I grew up in the 1970s and early 1980s, the language children spoke whenever they met was Hokkien, despite the introduction of the 'Speak Mandarin' campaign in 1979.

THE TRISHAW INDUSTRY AS A '*BANG*'-BASED TRADE

era. Indeed, 89 of them stayed in District 8 and another 56 in District 7. Two hundred and twelve trishaw riders were living in 12 streets – 13 at Desker Road and 17 at Bencoolen Street. The ten Henghuas, six Hokchias and a Foochow at Bencoolen Street were 'a little pot-pourri of Fukien province' (NAS, Transcript of A000117/09:40).[9] Seven trishaw riders lived at 40 Bencoolen Street, the premises of the SHTRA. Desker Road was almost certainly considered a Hokchia area as 13 Hokchia riders lived there in the early 1970s.[10]

Some trishaw riders conveniently chose to reside near or within entertainment and/or red-light districts. Lim Hong Cher would ride his trishaw along Joo Chiat and Geylang areas in eastern Singapore because he lived in that area. He would ride his trishaw every afternoon and earn about $8 (NAS, A000745/06, reel 1). The 17 who stayed at Desker Road provide another case. A distressed journalist named Sit Yin Fong considered Desker Road Singapore's 'Purgatory Lane', and considered it 'a picture of human tragedy' in 1954. Sit wrote that 'vice is cheap here' since 'a woman can be had for the price of three beers'. When a prostitute was summoned to a hotel, the trishaw rider would convey her to the rendezvous. Travelling expenses would be met by the client even if he did not like the appearance of the prostitute. As travel guides, trishaw riders also usually warned European sailors and soldiers to avoid the Desker Road area since the local people were particularly hostile to Europeans, believing they all were either police officers or someone connected with the colonial government (Sit 1983:103–110). Madam Lee Oi Wah, reminiscing on Chinatown in the 1950s, recalled that prostitutes used to travel in trishaws. To prevent themselves from being mistaken as prostitutes, other ladies would avoid sitting in trishaws unless they had children with them. Prominent prostitutes even had their own trishaw riders. Keong Saik Street (in Chinatown) was a red-light district and Madam Lee remembered many prostitutes who travelled on trishaws to their destination for business. The clients would call the prostitutes to go to certain places and they would travel in trishaws (NAS, A002217/09, reel 1).

The conditions of trishaw lodgings were usually poor. A *coolie keng* (workers' quarters) that was home to about ten trishaw riders at Ord Road in central Singapore had a dark interior with the only light coming from an opening located at the ceiling at the back of the shophouse (NAS,

---

[9] Fukien (Fujian) province is the home of the Henghuas, Hokchias, Foochows and, of course, the Hokkiens.
[10] See Appendices 5 to 8.

A002493/36, reel 15). Gamba also remarked about the case of a trishaw rider living in a single cubicle who had two wives and ten children. He took a second wife – a widow – because he wanted a male heir. His first wife had given him nine daughters. The concept that a large family might represent wealth and status was particularly important for that trishaw rider but even Gamba's illustration seemed uncommon (Gamba 1954:100–101). In 1947, the Singapore Housing Committee noted that 'the upper storeys [were] crowded with workers who eventually married and brought their families to live in the cubicles which were created' (Singapore Housing Committee 1947:5; Awbery & Dalley 1948:15 para 64). Overcrowding was a major problem of all houses in the inner city area. It was more likely, however, that the cubicles were usually shared by single riders, some of whom might be related to each other. There was no proper lighting and ventilation in most rooms except those facing the street. Most riders lived in rented premises and, while how much rent they paid per month could not be ascertained, an SWD survey in 1947 set the average rent for a cubicle at $9.60 per month and part of one at $2.95 per month (Department of Social Welfare 1947:4).

Life circumstances differed among the trishaw riders. Madam Foong Lai Kum remembered trishaw living quarters at 41 and 47 Sago Lane opposite her home in Chinatown. These quarters were popularly called *Che Zai Guan* or 'Trishaw riders' home'. There was a board at the front entrance that had the name of the owner of these quarters but the name *Che Zai Guan* was not there. Madam Foong recalled that most riders were in their thirties, but some were very old. Most of them were bachelors. If any of them fell ill, they would look after each other. Living conditions were terrible because they smoked and the quarters were smelly. Yet the trishaw riders looked after their own quarters, and would do spring cleaning before the Chinese New Year. The riders would have their meals outside the quarters because there was no space inside and there was no kitchen. The quarters had shared toilets and bathroom, and between 10 and 20 people would live there. Madam Foong remembered that the riders would rest after work and then wait in the mornings at markets for customers. At night, they would wait for customers at main roads or congregate after being contacted by tourist companies to bring tourists around Chinatown. Most of these riders, however, were Cantonese and they would communicate by hand signals if their customers were from other dialect groups. Most trishaw riders would park their trishaws outside *Che Zai Guan* at night as the streets had few cars and there were few hawker stalls. Madam Foong also remembered that the trishaw riders were sometimes drunk and would create din. Some of them were quarrelsome and some smoked opium (NAS, A002226/12, reel 8). Some trishaw riders could even afford to buy steamed buns for breakfast (NAS, A002935/CF1-2, disc 1). An elderly trishaw rider named 'Ah Tong' lodged with about 40 people in a *coolie keng* in the inner city itself. His room had both single- and double-decker beds but those who were hardworking and thrifty would eventually leave the *coolie keng*. Unfortunately for 'Ah Tong', who had been riding trishaws since 1946 and was still riding when I met him in 1995, he had gambled most of his savings away when he was a young man, leaving him 'too poor to find a wife' ('Ah Tong', interview, 12.07.1995).

Despite the poor living conditions, the earnings of a trishaw rider were high in the early 1950s compared with other occupations, as shown in Table 4 (Colony of Singapore Annual Report 1951:37; NAS, Transcript of A000117/09:49–51).

The amount earned, of course, depended largely on how long they had worked, the number of trips they had made and over what distance and time. Ng Kar Eng in his prime used to work 11 to 12 hours a day. He would start cycling at 5 am and return home at 6 pm. He could afford to work in this fashion since he owned his trishaw. There were times when Ng could pedal for 15 to 16 hours a day. On the other hand, a rented trishaw was usually only available to operate from 3 am to 3 pm the next day, although a rider could rent one for 24 hours if he wished to (NAS, Transcript of A000117/09:51). Similarly, 'Ah Tong' regularly worked 10 hours a day in the 1950s and 1960s. In 1995, when he was in his seventies, he still pedalled four hours a day ('Ah Tong', interview, 12.07.1995).

For some trishaw riders, the flexible working hours meant that they enjoyed a measure of freedom greater than those working in factories and shops. The riders had 'no superiors to please and no colleague to tolerate with' (Wee 1962:32). How much one earned depended solely on how hard he worked. Their income largely depended on fares collected over the course of a day. Under regulations laid down by the Municipal Council in January 1946, the fares were fixed at rates shown in Table 5. By the 1980s, however, with few passengers in a dying trade, the wages earned were so low the trishaw riders came to be regarded as occupying the lower income bracket in Singapore.

Interestingly, however, riders would usually charge more than the stipulated rate when carrying goods or produce even though it was an offence. Passengers, therefore, could bargain with the trishaw riders (NAS, B002294/09, reel 6). Bargaining, however, would not end cases of riders overcharging passengers. In November 1946, a writer to the forum page of

Occupation	Unit	Wages
Trishaw riders	Per day	$11 – $16
Bus drivers	Per day	$6 – $9
Glass blowers	Per day	$5 – $11
Laundry ironers	Per day	$5 – $6
Lightermen	Per month	$110
Compositors	Per day	$6 – $7
Rubber packers	Per day	$2.30 – $2.60
Sole gunners in rubber shoe factories	Per day	$1.50 – $3
Sawyers	Per day	$4

Table 4: Comparative wages of workers in various selected occupations in 1951

			$	c
By distance	For any half mile or fraction of half mile		0	20
By time	For one hour		1	50
	For every additional quarter of an hour		0	40
Detention	The hirer shall be entitled to detain the trishaw for 10 minutes for stopping at any place but for every hour or part thereof an hour during which any trishaw may be detained beyond the first 10 minutes an additional sum shall be charge-able viz.		0	25
	No rider shall be entitled to claim as payment for any distance travelled or any time during which he may be detained in any one day more than		6	00

Table 5: Rates of hire for trishaws

Sources: *The Straits Times*, 8 January 1946, p. 3; and The Municipal Ordinance No. S.447, 25 November 1948

The Straits Times noted that there were no fare cards displayed in the trishaw and so he/she did not know how much the fare really was. For a quarter mile ride, the rider demanded more than 30 cents. When the passenger refused to pay, 'the result was swearing and filthy language, with a call for a fight' (*The Straits Times*, 31.12.1946). Based on Table 5, the rider was clearly overcharging the passenger. By December 1946, new regulations were passed whereby all trishaws had to carry an official table of fares. Additionally, no trishaw would be registered if it did not have a bell, efficient brakes, and suitable front and rear lamps – or an approved reflector in place of a rear lamp. Also, every trishaw rider had to wear an arm badge with the number clearly visible.

THE TRISHAW INDUSTRY AS A *'BANG'*-BASED TRADE

The period immediately after World War II was the 'golden era' for the trishaw industry. Tan Ai Mai worked as a trishaw rider from 9 am to 3 pm in 1947 and he would earn between $10 and $20. If the day's work was not good, and he had to spend up to an hour waiting for passengers, then the day's earnings could drop to between $5 and $8 (NAS, A000132/05, reel 3). Occasionally during a literal ride, Ng Kar Eng would take a naive Allied soldier for a metaphorical 'ride' and be paid up to $20 for the trip. Ng said that so long as no one complained unduly, the local government authorities did not know about such practices, and he felt safe (NAS, Transcript of A000117/09:49–51.).[11] Ng earned about $15 a day between 1947 and 1954, although sometimes his daily takings were as low as $11. However, beginning in 1957, his income fell to an average of $10 per day. 'Ah Tong' recalled that in the 1960s he often earned between $3 and $4 per day. Trishaw riders could earn as much as $20 per day but to earn that amount, they had to travel to the marketplace at 4 am and transport goods and people from place to place on a huckstering round. While fares were set according to the Municipal Council schedule, depending on the weight of the market load transported, a fee from $1.50 to $3 could be charged. Thus riders who earned up to $20 per day hauled goods and produce more often than not, and such riders usually worked non-stop until 10 am ('Ah Tong', interview, 12.07.1995).

Ordinarily, the trishaws depend solely on human labour to move them around (Meier 1977: 116). A study conducted by Nanyang University in 1971 considered trishaw riding as exploitation of human labour and noted that it was not an occupation meant for the weak (Nanyang Daxue Lishi Xi 1971: 59–60). Riding a trishaw for years on a gruelling daily schedule often took its toll on the cyclist. While detailed medical evidence is unavailable as to whether they suffered major disabilities or diseases as a consequence of trishaw pedalling, Ng mentioned that riders often suffered cardiac problems and liver ailments because of trishaw riding. It appeared too that once a rider stopped pedalling, he found it 'difficult to walk'. Interestingly, Ng felt that rickshaw pulling did less damage to the human body than trishaw riding (NAS, Transcript of A000117/09:64).[12] Tay Quay Muay, however, felt that

---

[11] For an example of gullible foreigners who used the trishaws in Lucknow, India, see Gould 1965:29 (footnote 1).

[12] See also Warren, *Rickshaw Coolie*, Chapter 9 for a detailed discussion of morbidity and mortality among Singapore's rickshaw pullers; T H Thomas, *Rickshaws In Calcutta*, p. 32 about possible sexual impotence because of years of cycling; and Gould, 'Lucknow Rickshawallas', p. 43 found trishaw riders suffering from 'white leprosy' or severe emotional disturbance.

pedalling a vehicle was much easier than pulling one (NAS, Transcript of A000739/03:20). Lim Hong Cher, who rode a trishaw from 1956 to 1983, did not suffer any major ailments from his many years of trishaw riding (NAS, A000745/06, reel 6).

In terms of representation, trishaw riders protected their working and welfare interests through the SHTRA. Registered on 6 June 1950, the SHTRA took over the role and responsibilities of the SRTWU, which was de-registered on 10 June 1950. The Executive Committee of the SHTRA comprised 31 members; 14 ordinary members, two trustees and four co-opted members. The SRTWU had been a member of the pro-communist Singapore General Labour Union (GLU) but when the latter was superseded by the Singapore Federation of Trade Unions (SFTU), the SRTWU and its successor the SHTRA did not join the SFTU.[13] The trishaw riders were drafted into GLU branches after 1945 due to the strong influence of Chinese nationalism or communism during the Japanese Occupation (Stenson 1970:116; Awbery & Dalley 1948:25 para 101).

In terms of politics, the STOA was considered 'right-wing and capitalist' while the SHTRA was 'left-wing'. The SHTRA also tried to get trishaw riders who owned their own vehicles to join the association rather than the STOA. The rivalry between both STOA and SHTRA would also intensify when both sides presented their vehicles for inspection at the Registry of Vehicles (ROV) compound. The English Secretary of the STOA even tried to amalgamate both associations but had no success (NAS, A000280/20, reel 19).

A recurring issue between owners and riders was the rental charge. As early as September 1946, the owners tried to set a rental price of $3 per trishaw. The SRTWU (predecessor of the SHTRA) appealed to the Controller of Labour, asking his assistant to fix the rental prices of trishaws as well as giving to the SRTWU the authority to issue trishaw licences to the riders. Their petition could have met with sympathy from the then Controller of Labour, RH Oakeley, who noted that out of 5,000 trishaws in Singapore, there were 1,000 which were self-owned. Each trishaw would cost about $200 and could be hired for $3 each from 8 am to 6 pm. An agreement between the STOA and the SRTWU was eventually signed before Oakeley on 16 September. Under this agreement,

---

[13] For a list of unions affiliated to the GLU, see Gamba, *The Origins of Trade Unionism in Malaya*, pp. 462–463. For a list of unions affiliated to the SFTU, see Alex Josey, *Trade Unionism in Malaya* (Singapore: Donald Moore, 1954), pp. 96–105.

the rent for a trishaw was fixed at $1 for 24 hours with the hirer responsible only for the repair and change of tyres, as well as minor repairs such as replacing broken spokes. The owners, however, would be responsible for all other repairs except those resulting from damage caused by the hirers. Furthermore, the cost of the trishaw licence would be borne by the owner and he/she could no longer take the trishaw back from the hirer without giving the latter 14 days' notice. Similarly the hirer had to give the owner 14 days' notice should he decide to stop riding the trishaw (NAS, ML 897, RTU 55, 11.09.1946 & 16.09.1946).

A problem occurred later when some trishaw owners continued to hire out trishaws at $3 to $4 instead of $1 per day. The SRTWU lodged a protest with the STOA, but the latter insisted the riders were informed about the new rates. Trishaw riders were advised by the STOA to report such cases to the authorities as the STOA had no power to force the SRTWU to comply with the new rates (NAS, ML 1918, LM 238/46, undated memorandum).

In addition to representing trishaw riders in their disputes with the owners, the SHTRA also assisted riders by providing mutual aid and support, explaining government regulations and mediating on their behalf with the authorities. A SHTRA representative would always accompany a rider whenever the latter had to pay a fine for a particular municipal or traffic offence. The subscription was set at a dollar per member per month. However, in 1961, the Registry of Mutual Benefit Organisations (RMBO) ordered registration of the mutual aid section of the SHTRA. From then on, all members of the SHTRA had to pay 50 cents to the association and 50 cents to the newly created Singapore Hired Trishaw Riders Mutual Benefit Organisation (SHTRMBO). The SHTRMBO ensured that should a rider die from old age, illness or misadventure, his family or next-of-kin would receive $140 to cover burial fees (NAS, Transcript of A000117/09:67–68).[14] Like other mutual aid associations, the SHTRMBO was subscribed to by the riders to so that there would be adequate funds for their death rituals (Tong 1993:130). As far as the actual power and authority of the association in the daily lives of the trishaw riders was concerned, it acted as a bridge

---

[14] Ng was then the treasurer of the SHTRMBO as well. In a letter from K H Tan of the Registry of Mutual Benefit Organisations to the Secretary of the SHTRMBO dated 3 November 1962, however, the government ordered that the amount collected every three months for the SHTRMBO would go into the bank as SHTRMBO funds and withdrawals were allowed only when someone died (NAS, RMBO 1.328 and RMBO 1.328.2).

between local authorities and its often ill-educated members. Even then, not all trishaw riders saw the need to join the SHTRA. Tan Ai Mai felt it was a 'useless' organisation and so left it after a few years (NAS, A000132/05, reel 4).

Trishaw riders provided an important means of transport in the early post-World War II period, but despite their ability to jeopardise the overall transport system if they wished to do so, the trishaw riders never went on strike except during the BMA. At that time, the GLU staged a successful strike by port workers to obtain higher wages and this strike was then followed by similar strikes by other groups of workers. When employees of the Singapore Traction Company (STC), the government-run bus company, went out on strike in October, the rickshaw pullers and trishaw riders went on strike too. Gilmour wrote that they stopped work in sympathy with the STC employees and their concerted action paralysed the city's entire transport system. The following day, however, rickshaw pullers, trishaw riders and some bus drivers returned to the empty streets (Gilmour 1950:179; *The Straits Times*, 26.10.1945; *The Straits Times*, 27.10.1945; Stenson 1970:64–65). In December 1945, the rickshaw pullers and trishaw riders went on strike with other transport workers, although there was a report that 'thousands of rickshaw pullers and trisha riders who remained off the streets did so against their wishes'. Accusations of intimidation were made by the BMA but there was no investigation (*The Straits Times*, 28.12.1945).

In January 1946, the riders went on strike again in support of the call by the GLU for the BMA to release labourers and trade unionists and return properties of the GLU in Johor state in Malaya (*The Straits Times*, 30.01.1946; *The Straits Times*, 31.01.1946). After that, the riders never went on strike again, although they came very close to doing so in 1947. Many trishaw riders appear to have resigned themselves to their fate. When asked why they never went on strike as rickshaw pullers had done in pre-war Singapore, the common reply was 'What for?' If they did not work one day, it meant the loss of a day's income (NAS, Transcript of A000739/03:21; 'Ah Tong', interview, 12.07.1995). In the era of post-war recovery their association had neither the fighting fund nor the political will to sustain a large scale strike for an extended period of time.

Therefore, when another general strike by 4,000 bus workers in 13 bus companies occurred on 13 June 1955, the trishaw riders did not take part. They continued to ply the roads, picking up passengers who could not take the bus that day! Things, however, got worse as the days wore on. On 15 June, it was reported that 'all Singapore taxis were forced off the roads by intimidators yesterday as the organisers of the 'general strike' sought to strengthen their grip on the city'. By 9 am, there was hardly a taxi on the roads. It was feared that the trishaw riders could be forced off the roads by intimidators as well, causing housewives to put off their market shopping that day. But *The Singapore Tiger Standard* reported that 'trishas did a roaring business all day charging rates normally levied by taxis'! The same newspaper reported on 16 June that trishaw riders and some taxi drivers had apparently refused to be intimidated and continued to ride the streets of Singapore. It was also reported that the SHTRA was 'not unnaturally disgusted' when asked whether trishaw riders were staying away from the streets due to intimidation. The reply from SHTRA was, 'Any trishaws on the road? Have you no eyes to see?' (*The Straits Times*, 14.06.1955; *The Straits Times*, 15.06.1955; *The Singapore Tiger Standard*, 15.06.1955; *The Singapore Tiger Standard*, 16.06.1955)

The passing of a golden era

As noted, the Chinese community in colonial Singapore was not a monolinguistic group. It was divided by dialects, with members of each dialect group keeping to themselves in small enclaves in the city centre. The mutual unintelligibility of each dialect meant that when a member of a dialect group entered a particular trade, he/she would hire friends and apprentices from the same dialect group. Over time, that trade became associated with a dialect group or a *bang*. As the Henghuas and Hokchias came much later than the major dialect groups in the nineteenth century, they had no choice but to take up rickshaw pulling and reside in areas just outside the city centre. When the rickshaws introduced in 1880 were finally banned in Singapore in 1947, some of the pullers switched to trishaw riding. This development explains why the Henghuas and Hokchias – despite being minority Chinese dialect groups – could also dominate the trishaw industry in Singapore.

Since the trishaws fanned across the city centre, picking up passengers and providing that crucial (and appreciated) door-to-door service, the colonial authorities became concerned as to whether these riders could present a potential problem for the colony due to the large number of trishaws. The way the British went about trying to regulate the industry showed their suspicions of the industry. The SRTWU and its successor the SHTRA had large memberships. Regulations had to be brought in to ensure that there would not be major problems for the British from the unions. Fares had to be regulated in order to ensure that riders would not over-charge passengers. Correspondence between the colonial authorities and the union reveal that while the latter was very concerned about protecting the interests of its members, the British would prefer to avoid any contact with the union. For example, the union constantly alleged that there could be corrupt officials from the VRD who forced riders to part with their hard-earned money as bribes. The British side-stepped this issue rather than meet officials from the union for negotiations.

Trishaw riders in Singapore occupied one of the lower echelons of society. Their income was based on what they could earn in a day and they worked long hours. Many riders lived in rented premises. Most of the riders remained bachelors. The SRTWU and SHTRA could have used their numbers to demand better conditions but they never did so, except during their participation in two strikes in 1945 and 1946. The riders did so in support of the GLU. However, if they chose to go on strike, it meant a loss of income and as the living standards of the trishaw riders were generally poor, a loss of income would be extremely painful for the rider and, if he had one, his family. The problem of having to live hand to mouth every day was the reason that, despite their large numbers, most trishaw riders chose not to participate in the political activities that were unfurling around them in Singapore in the 1950s. The riders were powerless to obtain better working and living conditions for themselves. Unlike the 1940s when the rickshaws were a ubiquitous sight in the streets, the public preferred motorised transport in the 1950s. It was no wonder then that the SHTRA was considered a 'useless' organisation by Tan Ai Mai. The period just after World War II was the 'golden era' for the industry, as earnings were high, but by the 1960s it was clear that that era had passed.

Plate 1

Royal Navy non-commissioned officers C Latham and B Watson going sight-seeing in Singapore in a trishaw in 1945. The original caption of the photograph in the Imperial War Museum called the vehicle a 'taxicle' *(Courtesy of the Imperial War Museum)*

Plate 2

A trishaw park in Singapore in October 1945. *(Courtesy of the Imperial War Museum)*

Plate 3
Trishaws and rickshaws along Victoria Street on 1 October 1945. *(National Archives and Records Administration Collection, courtesy of the National Archives of Singapore)*

Plate 4
A trishaw rider and a rickshaw puller along Bras Basah Road on a very wet 15 April 1947. The days of the rickshaw pullers were numbered by then and many of them switched to trishaw riding once rickshaws were ordered off the streets on 1 May that year. *(Courtesy of the National Archives of Singapore)*

Plate 5
Kian Seng Heng Bicycle Trade at No. 37 Pagoda Street in Chinatown used to repair and maintain trishaws until it shifted to Tiong Bahru in June 1995. This photograph was likely to have been taken in the 1980s. *(Courtesy of the National Archives of Singapore)*

Plate 6
Mr Chan Chee Seng, Parliamentary Secretary in the Ministry of Social Affairs, attending the swearing-in ceremony of the Singapore Hired Trishaw Riders Association on 19 February 1966. Note that some riders were wearing their 'uniform' of a blue Nankin tunic and shorts. *(Ministry of Information, Communication & the Arts Collection, courtesy of the National Archives of Singapore)*

Plate 7

A meeting of the Singapore Hired Trishaw Riders Association on 7 January 1967. Note the ubiquitous 'soda-pop' bottles on the table. *(Ministry of Information, Communication & the Arts Collection, courtesy of the National Archives of Singapore)*

Plate 8

A representative of Nanyang University, Chuang Hui-Tsuan (right), awarding a silk banner of appreciation to Chng Keng Swee, President of the Singapore Hired Trishaw Riders Association, after 1,577 trishaw riders participated in a charity ride and raised $21,600.51 for the new Chinese university. *(Courtesy of the National Archives of Singapore)*

Plate 9
Trishaws lined up in the Registry of Vehicles before the charity ride for the National Defence Fund in 1968. *(Courtesy of the National Archives of Singapore)*

Plate 10
Chan Chee Seng (right, in white shirt), Parliamentary Secretary to the Minister for Social Affairs, receiving donations from members of the Singapore Hired Trishaw Riders Association to the National Defence Fund on 24 April 1968. *(Ministry of Information, Communication & the Arts Collection, courtesy of the National Archives of Singapore)*

Plate 11

Trishaws will be found where large numbers of people would congregate. In this photograph several trishaws would pick up passengers from the Jubilee Theatre at North Bridge Road in 1950. *(Courtesy of the National Archives of Singapore)*

Plate 12

A trishaw rider and his passenger at Robinson Road in 1950. *(Courtesy of the National Archives of Singapore)*

Plate 13
Trishaw riders waiting for passengers in 1953. *(Lim Kheng Chye Collection, courtesy of the National Archives of Singapore)*

Plate 14
A column of trishaws going across Coleman Bridge towards New Bridge Road in 1950. *(Courtesy of the National Archives of Singapore)*

Plate 17
Trishaw riders and their vehicles could be found even along the 'thieves' market' at Sungei Road in the 1950s, picking up passengers after they had made their purchase. *(Philip Gower Collection, courtesy of the National Archives of Singapore)*

Plate 18
Trishaw riders waiting for passengers outside Thong Chai Medical Institute in the 1950s. *(Courtesy of the National Archives of Singapore)*

Plate 19

Trishaws along Sago Lane in 1963. Known as 'Street of the Dead', this road was notorious for its death houses, undertakers' officers and coffin-making shops. Note an undertaker's vehicle in the left foreground. *(Courtesy of the National Archives of Singapore)*

Plate 20

Trishaws travelling alongside buses and cars at South Bridge Road in 1963. *(KF Wong Collection, Courtesy of the National Archives of Singapore)*

Plate 21

Trishaw riders waiting to pick up passengers outside South East Asia Hotel in the 1960s. *(KF Wong Collection, Courtesy of the National Archives of Singapore)*

Plate 22

Trishaws and cars competing for space in a congested road in the 1960s. *(Courtesy of the National Archives of Singapore)*

Plate 23
Trishaws appeared very frequently along East Coast Road in the 1960s due to major shops and markets. *(Courtesy of the National Archives of Singapore)*

Plate 24
A trishaw rider picking up a woman and her purchased goods in the 1960s. *(Courtesy of the National Archives of Singapore)*

Plate 25
K M Byrne, Chairman of the Singapore Tourist Promotion Board, and Chan Chee Seng, Parliamentary Secretary in the Ministry of Social Affairs, looking at trishaw stands at Cathay, Goodwood and Singapura Hotels on 2 November 1965. *(Ministry of Information, Communication & the Arts Collection, courtesy of the National Archives of Singapore)*

Plate 26

Trishaws outside dilapidated shophouses in 1977. *(Paul Piollet Collection, courtesy of the National Archives of Singapore)*

Plate 27
A trishaw moving in the wrong direction along a congested South Bridge Road in 1983.
(Courtesy of the National Archives of Singapore)

Plate 28
How a trishaw cuts across a busy road. After looking over his shoulder, the trishaw rider quickly turns right ... *(Photograph taken by author in 1995)*

Plate 29

... cuts across a busy Jalan Besar, and enters Desker Road. *(Photograph taken by author in 1995)*

Plate 30

Hock Sin Hin Chop in Joo Chiat Road was founded in 1949 by the late Ong Tuck Kin. At its peak, it used to own 200 trishaws. With the collapse of both the bicycle and trishaw industries, the shop expanded to include motorcycle repair as well as selling toy cars for young children. *(Photograph taken by author in 1995)*

Plate 31

An attempt was made by the Municipal Commission to introduce motor trishaws as early as August 1950. The Municipal Commissioners took it on a test-run on 24 August 1950, flanked by curious onlookers. *(Source: The Straits Times © Singapore Press Holdings Ltd. Permission required for reproduction)*

Plate 32

By 1958 trishaw riders were expected to ride only if they had registered themselves with the Registry of Vehicles. On 12 May 1958, this trishaw rider turned up at the ROV to get his new badge. Once he had received his badge, he was a licensed rider and could ride the trishaw in peace. *(Source: The Straits Times © Singapore Press Holdings Ltd. Permission required for reproduction)*

Plate 33

About 1,000 trishaw riders took part in a charity ride on 3 May 1972 in aid of the proposed Chung Hwa Free Clinic in Toa Payoh. Parliamentary Secretary to the Ministry of Social Affairs Chan Chee Seng (seated on the second trishaw on the right) started the ceremony. Madam Chan Choy Siong (right), a Member of Parliament, is seated in a trishaw pedalled by Sim Boon Wee, another Member of Parliament. *(Source: The Straits Times © Singapore Press Holdings Ltd. Permission required for reproduction)*

Plate 34

A lone trishaw rider cycling in a flooded Chinatown on 4 May 1959. *(Source: The Straits Times © Singapore Press Holdings Ltd. Permission required for reproduction)*

Plate 35

A woman with her shopping load taking a trishaw at the Tekka Market at Serangoon Road on 5 December 1971. *(Source: The Straits Times © Singapore Press Holdings Ltd. Permission required for reproduction)*

Plate 36

A trishaw rider was killed when a heavily laden two-and-a-half-tonne lorry went out of control and caused a seven-vehicle smash-up at the junction of Paya Lebar Road and Paya Lebar Way on 4 January 1979. The other five vehicles involved were another lorry, two taxis, a Mercedes Benz car and a motorcycle. The picture shows the mangled remains of the trishaw under the lorry. *(Source: The Straits Times © Singapore Press Holdings Ltd. Permission required for reproduction)*

Chapter 4

THE TRISHAW INDUSTRY AND SINGAPORE SOCIETY

The trishaw rider and the public

Warren has described the rickshaw puller as 'a man of a hundred faces' who 'always seemed to have so many roles to play in the life and circumstance of the people they pulled every day' (Warren 1986:151). In many ways, the everyday role of the trishaw rider proved to be the same as well. A trishaw rider often acted as a guide for tourists. He also brought clients to visit prostitutes and entertainers. He escorted women to and from markets, as well as delivering their foodstuffs. Many riders were also 'booked' by well-off families to send their children to and from school, and were paid handsomely in return. In an urban environment where motor cars were increasingly common, the trishaw still provided a means of getting around for ordinary people who had to travel through back lanes, along narrow streets and even on expressways. Koh Boon Chai, for instance, was of the impression that housewives tended to sit in trishaws because the trishaws could reach the entrance of markets and their homes. There was no such convenience from buses, and taxi fares were expensive. Trishaw riders also sent students and the elderly to their destinations as it was inconvenient to travel by bus in the 1950s (NAS, A002009/08, reel 7). Trishaws could readily negotiate the back alleys of shophouses as well – places which were perceived as part of an underworld by locals, where 'socially illicit' activities like gambling and prostitution often occurred (Ho & Lim 1992:50).

Furthermore, until the 1980s, the majority of Singapore Chinese still resided in the inner city area, especially Chinatown. In 1947, for example, about 74 per cent of the entire Chinese population resided in the city proper

(Del Tufo 1949:294–295). It is significant to note, therefore, that as more and more people moved into the new housing estates springing up all over the island, the urban-based trishaw industry slowly crumbled. As Lu Tian Lee reflected, the city itself used to be the place where money could be earned as many people lived there but it had since become 'very quiet' (NAS, A000669/16, reel 11). Even as early as 1954–56, in a survey of Upper Nankin Street, which used to be considered an inner city area, just 3 per cent of employed people went to work by trishaw. A quarter of these residents were trishaw riders themselves (Kaye 1960:199 & 204).[1] Trishaw riders could bring passengers anywhere in Singapore as there was no demarcation of territory by dialect group (NAS, A000132/05, reel 4).

There were trishaw parks in Singapore immediately after World War II. As the years went by, it became more common to see trishaws cruising the streets looking for potential passengers or stationing themselves outside major buildings and areas of entertainment. There were also trishaw riders who 'specialise' by carrying certain customers from fixed spots. For instance, a group of riders could station themselves outside the Citizenship Office and only pick up passengers from the Office to send them to the Supreme Court and back. The riders would also direct passengers to the proper counter upon arrival at either the Citizenship Office or Supreme Court (Wee 1962:76–77). In 1947, one 'SS Ong' complained in *The Straits Times* that since there were no vehicle inspectors outside cinemas and amusement parks, the riders did not bother to park their trishaws in neat rows and this had caused 'a great deal of obstruction' (*The Straits Times*, 04.01.1947).

Some riders also provided personalised services. Ng Kar Eng regularly brought food hawkers to the markets so they could buy their goods to prepare their wares daily. He usually worked early in the morning around Chinatown and even travelled as far away as Lavender Street, Kampong Bugis and Crawford Street, which lie outside the confines of the inner city area. Hawkers and even particular businessmen were regular customers. A hawker whom he knew in Hylam Street usually faithfully waited his arrival. Ng would pick him up and drop him at the 'Old Market' at Telok Ayer Street. He returned later loading the things purchased in the trishaw. The hawker would then proceed independently to his place of business at Victoria Street, while Ng would ride his loaded trishaw to that destination. Ng worked in this fashion from 5 am to about 9 am and usually earned about

---

[1] Shortly after the surveys were done, Upper Nankin Street disappeared from the street map of Singapore.

$8 for these trips, after which he would have his breakfast (NAS, Transcript of A000117/09:55–56). Lu Tian Lee also provided such a custom service in Singapore. During the late 1940s, a 'nice lady' would ask him to pick her up at a certain place the next day, and he did so accordingly. Trishaws were still a novelty then, and while fares were dearer than those of rickshaws, the woman obviously preferred travelling in the trishaw (NAS, A000669/16, reel 12). Lu was also responsible for sending children to school and looking after their welfare. He was paid 20 to 30 cents per trip by parents who had 'booked' with him. Lu would fetch the children to school and wait for them to enter the building proper before moving off. He felt the children were his sole responsibility as long as he was taking them to school. However, he also realised that by transporting children to school, he often missed the opportunity to pick up other fares. Furthermore, young children tended to be better behaved than older children. He particularly disliked the pupils of Chong Hock and Ai Tong Schools because of their constant misbehaviour while in his trishaw. In the end, he wanted to give it up but some parents offered to pay him a dollar extra. Considering himself 'greedy', he relented and continued conveying their children to school (NAS, A000669/16, reel 12).

Chan Kwee Sung recalled many trishaw riders living in the Duxton Road area. It was likely that these riders were Hui Ann Hokkiens. The Henghua and Hokchia trishaw riders lived in residences lining the streets of Little India. Therefore, the area these riders worked stretched from districts 1 and 2 in the inner city area all the way up to districts 7 and 8 just outside the municipal limits. Chan, however, also remembered many non-Chinese riders working in suburban areas such as Joo Chiat and Katong, where residents were provided with 'an inexpensive and convenient mode of transport from the bus stop to their doorstep of their landed property' (Chan 1995b:2; Nanyang Daxue Lishi Xi 1971:52). Madam Ong Chwee Lan also saw her trishaw riders regularly pick people up from the Malay kampongs (villages) in the Joo Chiat area and deliver them to the local bus stop (Ong Chwee Lan, interview, 14.07.1995). In 1978, it was reported that 'one often sees the trishaw riders gossiping amongst themselves at coffee shops, along street pavements etc'. If one needed a ride, 'you have only to attract the attention of one of the trishaw riders, ask if he would like to earn some money and "hey presto", you're on your way' (Raffles Institution Interact Club 1978). Searching for trishaw riders was not difficult.

Trishaw riders led more or less mundane lives. They rarely rode more than five kilometres per trip, but a rider was always 'tanned and rugged no matter how wizened a character he was' (Chan 1995b:2). However, there were times when trishaw riders would respond to the call of the community and/or state, and come out en masse for charity rides. They took part in three major events: the fund-raising rides for Nanyang University (1954), the National Defence Fund (NDF) in 1968 and the charity ride for Chung Hwa Free Clinic in 1972 to build a free hospital in Toa Payoh in central Singapore (Plate 33).

Fund-raising for Nanyang University

Nanyang University or Nantah[2] developed out of a concern on the part of influential merchants that Chinese high school students in Singapore and elsewhere in Southeast Asia had no Chinese-language university to further their education.[3] Chinese students who wanted a tertiary education had to go to China. However, after 1949, when the Communist Party took control of China, no more high school teachers were allowed to enter Singapore, which resulted in an acute shortage of such teachers. University graduates from the mainland were barred from entering Singapore by the British colonial authorities, fearing the spread of communism. To make matters even worse, the University of Malaya restricted entry only to students of English-medium schools (Ou 1992:2–5).

On 16 January 1953, at a meeting of the Supervisory Committee of the Hokkien Huay Kuan, the President of the association, Tan Lark Sye, proposed that the community establish a Chinese university to fulfil the needs of high school students and nurture future intellectuals within the wider society. The Chinese community was meant to raise $5 million for the Nanyang University Fund (henceforth the Fund) to enable the construction of the university. In response to Tan's call for the Chinese community to do all they possibly could to help establish the university, the SHTRA responded with a 'One Chinese, One Dollar' (*Yi Hua, Yi Yuan*) campaign in March 1953. Part of that fund-raising campaign involved a charity ride

---

[2] 'Nantah' is the Chinese abbreviation for Nanyang University (Nanyang Daxue), which in the old Wade-Giles system was spelt 'Nan-yang Ta-hsueh'.

[3] There were nine Chinese high schools in 1953: Chinese High School, Chung Cheng High School, Catholic High School, Yoke Eng High School, Nanyang Girls' High School, Nan Chiau Girls' High School, Nan Hwa Girls' High School, Chung Hwa Girls' High School and St. Nicholas Girls' School.

THE TRISHAW INDUSTRY AND SINGAPORE SOCIETY

scheduled for 20 April 1954 in which all members of the SHTRA would participate, a gesture which Tan felt strongly encouraged by (Nanyang Daxue 1956:368; Ou 1992:5).[4]

The deadline for registration of trishawmen who wished to participate in the charity ride was set for 15 April 1954. On that day, 305 riders registered and it brought the total of those taking part to 1,540. Each cyclist was given a small flag with the words *Wei Nan Da Yi Ta* ('Riding for Nantah') to be placed on the trishaw as well as a can for passengers to put money in. Two bicycle companies also promised free repairs to any participating trishaw that broke down on the day. Some trishaw riders did far more than was required. For instance, one rider gave $60 to the Fund, took part in the charity ride and donated five big packets of biscuits. Another rider took part in the ride and donated 10 dozen bottles of 'Green Spot' (a type of soft drink). On the day of the charity ride, these cyclists would ride from 6 am to 5 pm and their earnings would all go to the Fund. They would use their physical strength and skill to achieve something important for the future welfare of the community, and people were encouraged to give riders as much money as possible since their overall success would depend largely on the size of donations. Bargaining over fares was not allowed, and the STOA agreed to waive all rents for their trishaws on that occasion. On that day another 37 riders registered themselves at the last minute for the charity ride, bringing the total to 1,577 riders, including two Indians.

A representative of the Nantah Committee, Chuang Hui-Tsuan, flag in hand, sent off the trishaw riders at the SHTRA office in Bencoolen Street at 7 am, after giving a silk banner to the SHTRA in appreciation. On that day, 'Chinese millionaires laid aside their motor cars' and boarded trishaws instead (*The Straits Times*, 21.04.1954). The riders went all over the island including destinations such as Katong, Bedok, Changi, Hougang and Tanjong Pagar (*Lianhe Zaobao*, 29.05.1995).[5] The media, particularly the Chinese press, spent the entire day capturing unique moments in which various members of the Chinese community did their small share for Nanyang University. At 2.20 pm, Ko Teck Kin, President of the Singapore Chinese Chamber of Commerce (SCCC) – the de facto leader of the Chinese community – boarded a trishaw ridden by Chng Keng Swee, President of the SHTRA,

---

[4] All information on the charity ride in this chapter is taken from two Chinese newspapers, the *Nanyang Siang Pau* and the *Sin Chew Jit Poh*, from 16 to 23 April 1954, unless otherwise stated.

[5] Katong, Bedok and Changi are on the eastern part of Singapore, Ow Kang is in the northeast and Tanjong Pagar is in the south.

from Ko's office to the SCCC. The short trip of 10 minutes covered South Bridge Road, Pickering Street, and New Bridge Road, ending at the entrance of the SCCC building in Hill Street. Ko then ceremonially donated $100 for the fare. In another case, Woon Chin Sin, a teacher at Catholic High School, and his bride took a trishaw ride after just being married in a Roman Catholic church. The newlyweds donated $20 to the Fund.

At the end of the day, all of the riders parked their vehicles in a queue which stretched from Middle Road all the way to Waterloo Street, and returned their fund-raising cans to the SHTRA premises at Bencoolen Street. Forty-five Chinese high school students – young people who would benefit from the establishment of the university – and SCCC members were divided into ten groups to count the money. A total of $21,535.53 was collected with Lim Dow Yoke having earned the highest amount – $257.03. Interestingly, Chng Keng Swee only came in third with $106.30. Considering he received $100 from Ko, it was obvious that, as the newspapers reported, he was primarily riding around ensuring that the charity ride went smoothly.

Chng was particularly surprised to learn that while the rides were meant to start at 7 am, some trishaw riders were already moving about at 3 to 4 am. These early birds sacrificed their sleep to fetch hawkers and fishmongers to the markets in order to earn some money for themselves that day. They knew that after 7 am their earnings were dedicated to the Fund, so they worked early in order to earn some income that day. Obviously, their livelihood mattered a lot to them as well. Since they earned their wages by the day, it would not be fair to them to give their entire earnings from the donation ride to the Fund. Despite such initiatives, however, trishaw riders still donated their own hard-earned money to the Fund. One rider gave a sweat-soaked $10 bill to the Fund after the charity ride ended. Another rider, a Hokchia named Seah Neng Suan, also gave $10 to the Fund and he stated that 'it felt like I had donated a brick to Nantah's foundation' (*The Straits Times*, 01.06.1995).[6]

Interestingly, on 21 April, a 59-year-old trishaw rider named Yeo Koon Shih, who did not take part in the charity ride and 'regretted' not doing so, specially donated that day's income of $3.80 to *Sin Chew Jit Poh* to forward to the Fund. He had wanted to take part but missed the registration deadline and felt it his duty to give his daily income to the Fund through the

---

[6] *The Straits Times* mistakenly noted Seah as a Foochow. A check with the SFA in July 1995 found that he was a member of this Hokchia association. One of the office staff dismissed *The Straits Times* report of his dialect group as inaccurate.

Chinese newspaper. Riders such as Yeo who continued to give money to the Fund even after the charity ride finished helped increase the overall total to $21,660.51 (Ou 1992:6). The success of the charity ride sponsored by the SHTRA also encouraged other Chinese trishaw riders in Malaya to do likewise. On 24 April, the Chinese riders of Port Dickson held their charity ride that day. The following day, it was announced that Chinese trishaw riders in Malacca would do likewise in the future (*Sin Chew Jit Poh*, 24.04.1954; *Sin Chew Jit Poh*, 25.04.1954).

Different trishaw riders, however, came to view the charity ride and their role in it somewhat differently. Ong Hu Ah, Seah Neng Suan, Lu Tian Lee and Ng Kar Eng all had little or no education, but decided to take part in the charity ride so that Singapore Chinese students had a university to attend in the future. In other words, they felt a strong sense of civic duty and responsibility towards the younger generation of Singaporean Chinese. According to Ng, about 500 of the participating trishaw riders were not SHTRA members but rather those who responded through SHTRA newspaper ads about two months prior to the event. Tan Low Kee, however, participated as a consequence of communal pressure: only because other SHTRA members joined in the ride. He knew that a Chinese university was to be built but nothing else about the purpose of the day. Non-SHTRA members also participated in the charity ride. Although no longer a member of the SHTRA, Tan Ai Mai volunteered to ride because he wanted to do his part in raising the money for the new university (NAS, A000132/05, reel 4). All in all, the charity ride proved to be a great success (*Lianhe Zaobao*, 29.05.1995; *The Straits Times*, 01.06.1995; NAS, A000669/16, reel 12; NAS, Transcript of A000117/09:82–83; NAS, A000895/06, reel 5; Nanyang Daxue 1956:371).

National Defence Fund (NDF)

In August 1965, Singapore seceded from the Federation of Malaysia and in 1967, it was announced that National Service was compulsory for all able-bodied men above the age of 18. In early 1968, the Defence Minister Lim Kim San announced the establishment of an NDF 'to build up Singapore's defences'. The first cheque for $10,000 was donated by members of six Citizens' Consultative Committees, and by 9 February a total of $287,000 had been raised. By the end of the month, over $1.6 million was pledged (SYB 1968:3).

A SLOW RIDE INTO THE PAST

The SHTRA responded to the national call by organising a charity ride to raise funds for the NDF. The new Chairman of the association, Chua Ah Teng, announced after his re-election in February 1968 that the SHTRA would be asking its members to donate a day's takings to the NDF (*The Straits Times*, 12.02.1968). On 20 April, in a joint meeting of the SHTRA and the STOA, the SHTRA adviser Chan Chee Seng encouraged all trishaw riders to take part in the proposed charity ride for the NDF. The meeting set the registration deadline for interested riders on 21 April, and on 22–23 April donation cans and flags were to be distributed at SHTRA premises at Bencoolen Street. Cyclists would also be given coupons to sell as part of a competition among them. On 24 April all registered trishaw riders would begin the charity ride at any time in the morning until 6 pm, after which they would return their vehicles and cans at the VRD building in Middle Road. The STOA promised three brand new trishaws as prizes for the three lucky trishaw riders who managed to collect the most money. The donations would be counted by trishawmen who did not take part in the charity ride (*Sin Chew Jit Poh*, 23.04.1968).

In all, 895 trishaw riders participated in the charity ride on 24 April. They fanned out into the streets early in the morning and returned to Middle Road promptly between 5 and 6 pm. Chan acknowledged the valuable contribution of the trishaw riders despite some confusion in the overall running of the campaign, although no details were given publicly. The STOA Honorary President Lee Kai Teck gave the trishawmen one dollar per rider, while the STOA decided not to collect that day's vehicle rent from riders who took part in the fund-raising ride (*Nanyang Siang Pau*, 25.04.1968; *Sin Chew Jit Poh*, 25.04.1968).

There was far less media coverage of trishaw riders taking part in the NDF charity ride than had been the case for the Nanyang University ride 14 years earlier. The *Nanyang Siang Pau*, a newspaper founded by prominent merchant Tan Kah Kee in 1923, was known to cater to the dominant Hokkien business community, with its news largely dominated by the economy. It reported the charity ride but without any great detail. However, the *Sin Chew Jit Poh* did record at least one story about Aw Cheng Chye, nephew of Aw Boon Haw and Director of the *Sin Chew Jit Poh*. Aw Cheng Chye had already earlier donated $20,000 to the NDF. But at 10 am on 24 April, Aw got his workers and friends to assemble at Neil Road where ten trishaws came to pick them up. From there, the group travelled through Cantonment Road, Hoe Chiang Road, Tanjong Pagar Road, Craig Road and then back to Neil Road. When the ride was over, all placed sums of money in the donation cans except Aw, who put a cheque for $500 in a rider's can (*Sin Chew Jit Poh*, 25.04.1968).

It was never ascertained exactly how much the trishaw riders managed to collect and donate to the NDF as neither the *Nanyang Siang Pau* nor *Sin Chew Jit Poh* recorded the final figure. But *The Straits Times* noted that the amount was 'expected to exceed' $8,000. Following further donations by taxi owners and drivers, the NDF peaked at the four million dollar mark. Not surprisingly, Lim See Chow, Chairman of the Management Committee of the Tanjong Pagar Community Centre, rightly remarked that 'the man in the street are the ones [sic] who have been doing the most for the defence fund' (*The Straits Times*, 27.04.1968).

Public perceptions of trishaws and riders

Despite the overall contribution of the trishaw industry to Singapore society, public perceptions of trishaws and riders have been more or less negative. Furthermore, foreigners' perceptions of 'the man and the machine' have tended to foster an erroneous image of the 'exotic'. It is worthwhile here to highlight differences in poses of rickshaw pullers and trishaw riders in photographs and picture postcards. In pre-war Singapore, when store-bought photographs of rickshaw coolies were common, many pullers were asked to pose for the camera against a scenic 'tropical' background. Warren notes that 'misunderstanding was created in the eye of the camera by insensitive Europeans who approached the rickshaw puller as simply one more curio Singapore offered to the traveller' (Warren 1985:29–42; Warren 1986:31). However, many existing photographs of Singapore trishaw riders were not posed. The photographs featured in this book must have been taken when the trishaw rider(s) least expected it and without prior consent or knowledge.[7]

Nevertheless, one theme remains constant in virtually all photographs of pullers and riders: both rickshaws and trishaws were framed by photographers as part of a 'natural' urban landscape of a busy city. Many of these photographs did not focus on trishaws specifically but inadvertently included them as part of the overall streetscape, landscape or transport scene or, as usually was the case, part of the local environment of particular neighbourhoods in Singapore. One gets the impression reviewing these photographs that some photographs tended to create a stereotypical image

---

[7] That is not to say that the trishaw riders never posed for the camera.

of trishaw riders and/or Singapore street scenes. It has been noted that 'all photographs had an audience in mind', and in the case of some images, 'the photographer(s) paradoxically chose to focus on unchanging representations of peoples and cultures. For it was the 'exotic', the culturally different, which fascinated' (Scherer 1992:35; Mydin 1992:249). Virtually all the photographs reproduced in this book conveniently gloss over the nature of the trishaw riders' strenuous livelihood; the physically difficult task of ferrying someone around, and other possible personal ethical issues which concerned the riders and passengers themselves. The result: a record of pictorial images and photographs which 'are often at variance with reality by ignoring the harshness of life behind the facade of the dream' (Cooper 1991:18).

The introduction of the trishaw during the Japanese Occupation led to a sudden expansion of the industry at the expense of rickshaws. Plate 2 depicts a trishaw park with two seemingly endless rows of vehicles in October 1945. The initial euphoria over the Japanese surrender had just died down, and life in the city was slowly picking up. Still, the widespread introduction of this man-powered vehicle merely created yet another 'ethnographic oddity' (Warren 1986:31) for European travellers and tourists in search of an 'exotic East' created by and for themselves. The two British servicemen seen posing in a trishaw in late 1945 (Plate 1) already testifies to the fact that the trishaw was the common mode of transport then. This was a time when 'streets in town were never free of smiling and fun-loving soldiers and sailors who always seemed loaded with chocolates which they felt free to hand out to children' (Chan 1995b:1). But as Barthes has noted, 'the photograph does not necessarily say *what is no longer*, but only and for certain *what has been*' (Barthes 1984:85).[8] A photograph may prove indispensable for an ethno-historical study of a particular aspect of Singapore's past but one should remember that the original purpose of some photographs was to represent a Singapore streetscape as an 'exotic' place. The servicemen here stage-posed in the eyes of the camera, and the smiling trishaw rider, seemingly almost welded to the trishaw itself, was rendered powerless and/or dehumanised in the process.

With the image of the trishaw firmly embedded in Westerners' minds as part of an urban 'exotic East', a glance at travellers' accounts and travel guides for Singapore provides some evidence of the ubiquitous trishaw existing to serve the needs of visiting tourists. Many of these descriptive accounts mention trishaws as part of local street scenes only in passing. The

---

[8] Emphasis in the quote was in the original text.

one exception is the lengthy, almost comical, description by Nancy Britton of a 1956 trishaw trip in Singapore:

> The way we happened to buy a car so soon was that we took a ride in a trishaw. A trishaw is a rickshaw attached to a bicycle (that's what I said), and there in one handy little contraption is combined the worst of two worlds. The driver rides the bicycle and the passengers ride a little green sidecar with a frilled hood on red spokes. A trishaw may have such accessories as shiny brass rails, chintz cushions, and Model-T rain curtains, but it never has springs, and you can record every cobble of the road using your spine as pedometer. In traffic it is a worse menace than an ox-cart, since trishaw drivers think faster than oxen and can do terrible things more unexpectedly.
>
> But we didn't know any of this. This particular afternoon we were down in the Chinese quarter on an errand. There were no taxis in sight, but there were plenty of trishaws and the *haute monde* of the district seemed to be bucking them with great aplomb, so the cosmopolitan Britons hailed one too and climbed in. Or we tried to. I could just fit my head under the awning with the frill over my face, but Frank wasn't so lucky. He sat sway-back with his shoulders braced outside the awning and his head somewhere up in the sky, and as our entourage jerked past, merchants stopped eating rice at the doors of their shop, hawkers stopped hawking, cards games on the pavement were abandoned, and everyone just enjoyed us. We got out at Raffles Place, flagged a taxi, drove to Orchard Road, and bought a car (Britton 1956:32–3).

This blunt satirical description of the trishaw in the 1950s portrays it as quite small and uncomfortable for Europeans. Britton's candid account is one of the few travelogues where the Singapore trishaw is described in great detail. Another unflattering description was provided by Patrick O'Donovan in 1950; he noted that 'there are many different designs, but they are all flimsy and uncomfortable' (Moore 1956:270–271).[9] Ronald McKie wrote about trishaw riders who 'pedalled their heavy clumsy vehicles with *three times the effort* that any despised rickshaw boy ever pulled' (McKie 1963:6).[10] During

---

[9] Obviously, this remark was written before it became compulsory for all trishaws to be painted green.
[10] Emphasis added.

the 1950s, George Peet, editor of *The Straits Times*, also similarly warned that 'in Singapore the trishaw is on its way out; it is hardly safe in the dense city traffic, and it is sometimes rather grubby' (Murdoch University Library, Peet Collection, File VI, undated).

The rhetoric of most other writings about trishaws and riders often contains stereotypical imagery which represents the rider as an inhuman figure more or less attached permanently to his vehicle. The cyclist and vehicle were often contrasted with a swift animal in order to highlight the supposedly slow speed of the trishaw. Patrick Anderson, for example, when writing about his experiences in Singapore in 1955, noticed 'a trishaw wheeling by with that special tigerish slowness of theirs (tigerish because of the gleam of brass)' (Anderson 1955:54). The 'brass' here referred to the spokes which held up the yellow-coloured hood of trishaws in Singapore.

However, there were occasional accurate observations about trishaw riders occupying the lower end of the socio-economic ladder in Singapore. The work of trishaw riders fitted the image of a hard, unspecialised blue-collar occupation, as the rider only had to know how to cycle properly. Peet, for instance, put it this way: 'In the eyes of the Singapore people, the trishaw is also not quite respectable' (Murdoch University Library, Peet Collection, File VI, undated). A letter to the forum page of *The Straits Times* in April 1946 asked, 'Are Singapore's trishaw-drivers recruited exclusively from homes for the mentally defective?' The writer – using the pen-name 'PAMM' – had found that several trishaw riders did not even know where key buildings in Singapore were located and concluded that 'clearly none of them has ever heard of a single place-name in the city where they work' (*The Straits Times*, 29.04.1946). The riders knew how to pedal but some seemed to have gotten themselves lost in the city.

Van Cuylenburg also recalled that after the Japanese surrender, there were 'innumerable' trishaws in Singapore cycled by 'really fierce-looking, truculent Chinese' (Van Cuylenburg 1982:256). Interestingly, the 'fierceness' of trishaw riders – coupled with the stereotypical image of the Henghuas and Hokchias as being both militant and rude – did not deter in any way some commentators from using the trishaw and abusing the rider. Swinstead and Haddon, writing about trishaw riders in 1981, suggested that passengers should not be bothered about the welfare of the rider:

> Apart from the attraction of the actual trishaw, there is the personality of the often frail-looking but nevertheless wiry rider moving the wheels as you embark on your motorless ride into history. *Do not feel sorry for*

> him as he struggles with the pedals. *It is his life, his job; he knows nothing else* ... They will greet you with broad smiles, baring their own private bank vaults of gold. *Their legs have given them all the wealth they require* (Swinstead & Haddon 1981:20).[11]

However, the actual life and circumstance of trishaw riders, as examined in the previous chapter, was often a harsh one. And they were never wealthy despite the odd gold tooth filling. This image effectively 'sanitised and divorced [the speaker] from any association with the poverty that marks the lives of people in the places that modern travellers often visit' (Albers & James 1988:153).

Few bothered to see the dangers of the trade. One writer, who did see the dangers of trishaw riding, placed the risk of death as shared equally between the trishaw rider and his passenger:

> Trishas are found in every Eastern city and are basically tricycles. The name is a corruption of the human-drawn ricksha which is now more or less abandoned in the interests of humanity ... There are various designs, no city using more than one design. In Bangkok the driver sits in front and the passenger behind; in Penang the position is reversed. In Singapore and Djakarta they travel side by side, driver and passenger, *thus taking the equal risk of being killed* (Moore 1954:76).

The danger of trishaw riding is evident when we consider the traffic accidents involving the trishaw riders. Trishaw riding was not a mere 'motorless ride into history' (Swinstead & Haddon 1981:20) – the life of the trishaw rider was at stake every time he plied the streets. An average of two deaths involving cyclists and trishaw riders were recorded every month in 1982. The riders were blamed for taking short cuts by riding against the flow of traffic, disregarding traffic light signals and switching lanes without signalling (*The Straits Times*, 09.08.1982). Yet, there were also instances when trishaw riders were killed as a result of a head-on collision with vehicles that had gone out of control. On the day Singapore launched Safety First Week in May 1947, a fatal accident occurred involving a lorry and a trishaw along Thomson Road. By 1949, there was a call for trishaws to be banned in the city centre, with a writer to *The Straits Times* forum page complaining that there

---

[11] Emphasis added. 'Private bank vaults of gold' refer to the riders' gold-coloured teeth that replaced lost teeth.

were 'too many' trishaws and that he/she considered it 'safer to travel by taxi than by trishaw' (*The Straits Times*, 29.09.1949). In January 1979, a trishaw was hit by a lorry and dragged along the road, killing the rider instantly. The heavily laden two-and-a-half tonne lorry had gone out of control and caused a seven-vehicle smash-up at the junction of Paya Lebar Road and Paya Lebar Way in northeastern Singapore (*The Straits Times*, 05.01.1979).

Some comments about trishaw riders could be insensitive. McKie, for instance, remarked confidently that 'a trishaw ride can be fun, *even for the rider*' (McKie 1972:15).[12] Few travellers' accounts actually considered whether the labour of trishaw riders was exploited, from a humanitarian standpoint; there was no reason to do so as it was the riders' job to simply convey tourists and locals to wherever they wanted to go in Singapore, irrespective of the weather or time of day. Even *The New Nation*, an afternoon paper from the 1970s up to the early 1980s, noted that 'it is not just for fun that tourists take a ride in a trishaw in Singapore'. The newspaper concluded that 'for most it is for the experience, to sample a unique feature which is absent in their homeland'. Trishaw riders would be asked to pose for photographs and 'normally' compensated S$1 or S$2 'for a few moments of fun and experience for the tourists' (*The New Nation*, 09.09.1971).

The local population also tended to be divided with respect to their views about the trishaw industry. On the one hand, trishaws provided an important means of public conveyance, but on the other hand it could also be readily perceived as a nuisance or a case of one human being exploiting the labour of another. In April 1947, for example, a reader wrote to *The Straits Times* that there were too many trishaws on the roads, and that 'some of them create a deafening din by ringing their bells continuously and unnecessarily'. He also complained that 'others drive recklessly and when they bump into pedestrians they curse as if they own the roads' (NAS, ML 1918, LM 238/46, 24.04.1947).

Oral recollections revealed people's perceptions of the trishaw industry as the years went by. Mrs Rita Fernando remembered fondly that two people could squeeze into a trishaw 'if you are not too fat' (NAS, A002044/08, reel 6). Richard Tan remembered the trishaws in the Katong area in eastern Singapore as follows:

> Whether it's going to Queen's cinema to see a movie or it's going to Geylang Serai ... those movie houses in those old days, or going to

---

[12] Emphasis added.

Roxy and Palace, on the other end with Odeon-Katong ... It's very cheap. I can still remember it's something like 30 cents just to hop on a becak [trishaw]. It's what makes it special and today we have lost that call greatly. It's gone, you know. And I only wish people can do that – just step out and flag down a becak and then just say 'Stirling Road' or 'Lorong Stangee' or you think of Sea Avenue or you want to go visit somebody. It's just so easy, you know. It's different, it's not the same when we take a taxi. It's not the same when you take a bus. So it's the ambience. When you sit, it's the open air, the wind is blowing in your face, and you are just going from place [to place]. And when you see someone you know on the road, you actually wave, you know, and you say 'hi, hello' (NAS, A002108/08, reel 4).

Another interviewee, Lim Tiang Lin, also remembered watching movies on Saturdays at Roxy Cinema in Katong. He, too, would go to the cinema by trishaw with his friends. In fact, he recalled spending 30 to 50 cents as fare and up to three or four people would squeeze into the trishaw (NAS, A001870/12, reel 1). There were also incidents when passengers tried to escape paying the fares (NAS, A000745/06, reel 6).

Wee Jong Dit, in his own recollection of the Joo Chiat area in the 1950s, mentioned that trishaws were common at Joo Chiat Market as not everyone owned a car. People would travel to and from the market by trishaws. However, trishaws could only travel short distances, and on fixed routes. It seemed that trishaws could go all the way to one's home, but most people would rather alight from the trishaws a short distance from their homes as they did not trust the trishaw riders and did not want the riders to know where they lived. Wee remembered the fare of $1 which was the price of being ferried from Geylang Serai to Joo Chiat (NAS, A002028/14, reel 5). In 1971, an article in *The Straits Times* mentioned the work of a 62-year-old trishaw rider who had been sending the mail for Mansfield and Company (Pte) Ltd for the last 15 years, without complaint. Through this 'one-man trisha mail service', Seow Sar Lui could earn some extra income to support his family and provide an education to his six children.

Carstens is of the opinion that trishaw riders were 'underemployed' in Singapore by the mid-1970s (Carstens 1975:15–16). Obviously, she did not treat trishaw riding as a mainstream urban occupation in her analyses. Interestingly, Ng Kar Eng's daughter shared a similar attitude and outlook. Upon becoming a seamstress, she tried to persuade Ng to quit trishaw riding even though he was then a permanent staff member of the SHTRA as its treasurer. She considered trishaw riding in the 1960s as demeaning in much the same way as 'today's people'. Ng was quite upset about his daughter's one-sided views, insisting that trishawmen were just doing their job and not generally robbing or cheating others (NAS, Transcript of A000117/09:63). Even an ex-trishaw rider like Ong Hu Ah, while recollecting his role in raising funds for Nantah in 1954, noted that since trishaw riders were generally looked down upon, as occupying the bottom rung of the socio-economic ladder, it was hoped that the charity ride would not prevent the public from doing their charitable bit for Nanyang University (*Lianhe Zaobao*, 29.05.1995). Tan Ai Mai felt that although some people looked down on trishaw riders, he had no choice but to continue riding his vehicle as there was no other work for him and he had no money to start his own business (NAS, A000132/05, reel 5).

Obviously, there were trishaw riders who knew what people thought of them but they chose to grin and bear it in silence. While he was still a rickshaw puller, Tay Quay Muay remembered some Malays calling him a 'Chinaman'. Even though he did not know what the term meant, he realised instinctively that it was a derogatory remark. Tay felt that so long as he did nothing wrong, it was better for him to work in a harsh prejudiced environment and yet remain a decent hardworking person (NAS, Transcript of A000739/03:16).

Alleged misbehaviour of trishaw riders

As the number of trishaws and riders increased with the ban of rickshaws on 30 April 1947, there was a corresponding increase in the number of reports on how trishaw riders were linked with inconsiderate behaviour and even criminal activities. Wee Jong Dit recalled that the trishaw riders then had a 'bad reputation', as it was common to see them fight, and talk in an uncouth manner. Wee felt that people in the area seemed to think that the trishaw riders fought over small matters, and therefore they refused to instruct the trishaw riders to go all the way to their homes unless they were carrying a heavy load (NAS, A002028/14, reel 5). By the 1980s, the public came to view trishaw riders with suspicion and frustration. As Singapore developed a modern showcase image, people's attitudes towards what constituted a 'decent' occupation changed, and trishaw riding came under increasing public scrutiny. Unfortunately, the lives of trishaw riders

THE TRISHAW INDUSTRY AND SINGAPORE SOCIETY

tended to be portrayed in a negative light. Trishaw riders were usually seen to be linked to prostitution, gambling and other social problems. A 1971 Nanyang University survey, for instance, found that many riders acted as pimps. Many of them refused to reveal how much they earned from pimping (*The New Nation*, 29.01.1971). Cheng also quotes a source which alleged that many Foochows and Henghuas had a tendency to play tontine (Cheng 1985:111–112). Lu Tian Lee also recalled that some trishaw riders risked gambling by tontine in order to buy a second-hand trishaw as early as 1946 (NAS, A000669/16, reel 11). In 1982, a university professor claimed to have 'unmasked' certain trishaw riders who extorted money and, perhaps, regularly overcharged passengers (Qiu 1990:93).

In May 1947 it was reported that attempts to register trishaw riders were unsuccessful because of the presence of posters in the streets threatening any trishaw owners who dared to register their vehicles with the VRD (NAS, ML 1918, LM 238/46, 26.05.1947). In June, an unknown organisation called the 'Singapore Trishaw Riders Committee' placed posters around Chinatown, threatening any trishaw rider who wore an arm badge with death. One poster suggested that the arm badge was an attempt by the colonial authorities to control labour (*The Straits Times*, 11.06.1947). The issue of registering trishaws and wearing arm badges had taken a brief sinister turn. It was suggested that the threats were made by those trishaw riders with secret society links, but nothing conclusive was reached (NAS, ML 1918, LM 238/46, 14.06.1947). A few days later, a writer to *The Straits Times* named 'Peace Lover' condemned the trishaw riders' behaviour as 'typical of their threats to civilians' and called for the riders to be tested on the English and Malay languages and their knowledge of the city. 'Peace Lover' alleged that 'many of the trishaw fraternity are members of secret societies' and 'they are a high-handed lot – these trishawmen' (*The Straits Times*, 14.06.1947). Furthermore, he/she recounted how a passenger was assaulted by a trishaw rider outside Jubilee Theatre along North Bridge Road, and 'told to pay better next time' (NAS, ML 1918, LM 238/46, 14.06.1947). The crimes went unsolved.

When two inspectors from the VRD told ten trishaw riders to move away from the entrance to Clifford Pier, they were beaten up by the riders. It was reported that 'the assault on the inspectors was an indication of lawless tendencies among a group of trishaw riders in Singapore' and that VRD inspectors had received threats of assault as they attempted to take down the registration numbers of riders who had allegedly committed an offence (*The Straits Times*, 05.08.1947).

A SLOW RIDE INTO THE PAST

In February 1948 'An Observer' wrote to *The Straits Times* that the colonial authorities should crack down on a 'trishaw-women parade', as licensed trishaw riders were ferrying prostitutes along Stamford Road in the city (*The Straits Times*, 07.02.1948). Trishaw riders were also accused of the 'arrogant flaunting of traffic rules' (*The Straits Times*, 14.02.1948). In response, the Legislative Council empowered the Municipal Commission to prohibit the use of trishaws in particular streets, although the report did not mention precisely which streets (*The Straits Times*, 18.10.1948). From the 1940s to the 1980s, trishaw riders were reported to have been hauled to court for smuggling rice, gun possession, smoking opium, assault, theft, drug addiction and trafficking, vagrancy, running a brothel, using rude words, overcharging, fighting, extortion, rape and murder (*The Straits Times*, 03.12.1946, 25.04.1947, 05.07.1947, 03.08.1947, 15.08.1947, 09.06.1949, 03.02.1951, 28.06.1951, 09.12.1960, 28.04.1972, 11.01.1973, 25.04.1973, 27.12.1974, 14.06.1975, 18.06.1976, 17.04.1979, 26.10.1981, 03.01.1982, 15.02.1982, 20.09.1982 and 22.09.1982). Some trishaw riders who worked in areas where vice was common were known to be secret society members. They would not only extort money from hotel keepers and prostitutes but also riders who were non-members and wished to work in these areas. There were riders who 'specialise' in prostitution by bringing customers to certain hotels and brothels. Apparently, these riders would get a cut of the business. If the price was $10, the prostitute would keep $6 and the hotel keeper and trishaw rider would get $2 each (Wee 1962:77–78). Trishaw riders were also accused of bringing tourists to 'smut shows' where pornographic films would be screened (*The Straits Times*, 20.10.1973).

Public complaints against the trishaws rang loud and clear in the early 1970s. The Housing and Development Board (HDB), for instance, received complaints from residents of housing estates that trishaw owners and riders were parking irresponsibly. The HDB decided to collect data on parking problems faced by trishaw riders in housing estates (*The Straits Times*, 28.05.1975). In July 1975, the HDB told almost 300 trishaw riders in all its housing estates to park the trishaws in areas where they would not obstruct common passageways (*The Straits Times*, 05.07.1975). An annoyed writer named 'Pedestrian' wrote to the forum page of *The New Nation* on how trishaw riders 'seem to take pride in going the wrong way in a one-way street' (*The New Nation*, 27.11.1974). Complaints were also sent to the Ministry of Communications on trishaws fitted with loudspeakers and trishaws causing traffic congestion (NAS, CI 307, RV 443/5-11, 07.05.1976). There were even complaints that seemed rather vague, such as 'excessive noise' caused by trishaw riders (NAS, CI 307, RV 443/5-11 Vol 2, 14.05.1976). Public opinion had begun turning against trishaws and trishaw riders.

Newspapers also began reporting cases of inconsiderate behaviour by trishaw riders. In November 1974, *The Straits Times* wrote about 'trishaw riders who flirt with death' because they had taken short cuts against oncoming traffic (*The Straits Times*, 01.11.1974). That same month, *The New Nation* took a photograph of a trishaw rider and several cyclists who exercised a 'blatant disregard of the law' by going in the wrong direction at a one-way street (*The New Nation*, 30.11.1974). In September 1975, *The Straits Times* also published an article on how trishaws continued 'to have the freedom of the pedestrian mall' at Raffles Place even though a 'NO ENTRY' sign was clearly displayed (*The Straits Times*, 18.09.1975).

There was, however, a measure of public sympathy for the plight of the trishaw riders. The editorial of *The Straits Times* in October 1951 asked:

> Have you ever known a trishaw rider as an individual human being? Or do you just see him as one of a series of robots trundling through the streets? If you are a motorist, do you ever have anything but abuse for the trishaw rider? (*The Straits Times*, 12.10.1951)

The public appeared to have forgotten that there were trishaw riders who were themselves victims of crime. In September 1964, just two months after racial riots had broken out in Singapore, a trishaw rider was stabbed to death in his trishaw at Geylang Serai on the eastern part of the island. To prevent further racial clashes, riot police patrolled the streets and residents were ordered to stay indoors (*The Straits Times*, 03.09.1964). In 1971, a 47-year-old trishaw rider was stabbed as he fought off two armed robbers (*The Straits Times*, 16.11.1971).

Role of local and state governments

In the late 1940s, as Singapore began a programme of rebuilding the country after the devastation of war and the Japanese Occupation, the Municipal Commission took charge of local affairs in the city. Since trishaws were first introduced during the Japanese Occupation, the Commission was unable initially to tackle the problem of proliferating numbers of trishaws as there were no by-laws to govern these vehicles. All the Commission had on the books was Part XIII of a 1937 Municipal Ordinance which dealt with horse carriages, carts and rickshaws (Walters 1937:375–415). In August 1946, in response to a call by Commissioner SF Ho for enforcement of use of rear lights on trishaws, the President of the Municipal Commission stated that it could not be done as there were no by-laws governing trishaws. Therefore, for reasons of expediency and in recognition of the growing presence of trishaws, 'for the purposes of public transport trishaws are rickshaws' (NAS, NA 441, MPMCS, Minutes of a General Committee Meeting. 16.08.1946). This pragmatic interpretation was used so that Part XIII of the Ordinance could be enacted against trishaws.

The maiden attempt to regulate the trishaw industry was undertaken in December 1946. The Trisha (Registration and Licensing) Regulations of 1946 clearly stated the physical dimensions of the trishaw, the registration and licensing of riders, license fees, penalties, and passenger limits, as well as the use of efficient brakes and rear lights, and keeping a trishaw riders' registration book by the Registrar of Vehicles (CSGGS, S277, 21.12.1946). These regulations became by-laws in December 1948 and were confirmed in January of the following year. The by-laws contained the same regulations as the previous code, except that the height of the trishaw was increased by 6 inches. However, several additional regulations were included as well – trishaws could not carry advertisements; riders had to wear a standard set of clothes; public trishaw stands were to be regulated; and riders could neither smoke nor spit whilst pedalling (CSGGS, S36 of the Municipal Ordinance, 08.12.1948).

Once the trishaw regulations were put in place in 1946, local and state authorities sought to gradually reduce the number of trishaws and riders in Singapore. The efforts of the British colonial authorities represented by the Municipal Commissioners, in fact, were far more explicit about the question of traffic control and trishaw regulation than the PAP Government elected in 1959. In October 1946, the Commission initially agreed not to limit the number of trishaws plying the streets, but the riders had to be taught traffic rules (MPMCS, Minutes of Meeting of Committees Numbers 1 and 3, 16.10.1946). In April 1947, Commissioner Rajabali Jumabhoy proposed that trishawmen be tested on traffic regulations because 'we had seen trishaws weaving in and out between cars' (Jumabhoy 1970:135). On 27 April 1947, the Sunday Tribune carried a report that the Registrar of Vehicles believed that 'the saturation point will be reached soon' as there were 8,500 trishaws plying the roads of Singapore. While he maintained that the trishaws did not contribute to traffic congestion, he admitted their interference with traffic. He also reported that trishaw riders would be given licences once they passed the road tests (NAS, ML 1918, LM 238/46, 27.04.1947).

Jumabhoy's proposal was accepted and the first trishaw riders' tests were conducted in June that year. All current and prospective riders had to take the test by 31 August 1947. It was felt that the speed of the trishaw and the recklessness with which some of the trishaws were ridden posed a danger on the roads. Therefore, all trishaw riders would be tested on controlling the trishaws, road sense, knowledge of hand and light signals, and rates of hire (*The Straits Times*, 14.05.1947). The trishaw riders could pick up application forms from the Bencoolen Street Inspection Yard of the VRD, and a time and date for the road test would be given. Each trishaw rider had to present two photographs of himself and a trishaw (NAS, ML 1918, LM 238/46, 14.05.1947). The test would require the trishaw rider to ride his vehicle from the test site at Bencoolen Street to Bras Basah Road, enter Prinsep Street, and return after entering Middle Road. The test usually only lasted 10 minutes and those who passed received a license and an arm badge. Those who failed could take a re-test after one week, and if they happened to fail again, could still be re-tested after another 14 days (*Nanyang Siang Pau*, 03.06.1947; *Sin Chew Jit Poh*, 03.06.1947). A trishaw rider would then have to pay $6 for a license that had to be renewed within a year (NAS, A000745/06, reel 1). On 1 June 1947, a reported 250 trishaw riders took the road tests. Once they passed, they had to pay for a licence and wear their arm badges when plying the roads of Singapore. There were about 1,200 trishaw riders waiting to take the road tests, and at a rate of 275 riders per day, it was estimated that it would take three months to complete the road tests for 20,000 trishaw riders. The deadline remained fixed on 31 August (NAS, ML 1918, LM 238/46, 02.06.1947).

Trishaw riders were generally unhappy about wearing an arm badge. On top of that, they now also had to wear a standard blue uniform and go barefoot. According to Lu Tian Lee, the authorities initially wanted the riders' arm badge number to be also written on the backs of their shirts. The SRTWU successfully got the authorities to change its mind on this particular measure in the dress code, but it also quarrelled bitterly with the VRD over the compulsory wearing of an arm badge. As early as May 1947, the SRTWU wrote to the President of the Municipal Commission to voice its opposition to the wearing of arm badges. It argued that as trishaw riders were already paying $6 in taxes per quarter and a security deposit of $5, purchasing arm badges would be a further financial burden. It also questioned the Municipal Commission on why trishaw riders had to wear arm badges when rickshaw pullers did not do so? (NAS, ML 1927, LM 272/47, 27.05.1947).

The SRTWU also implied that payment for arm badges was one way for corrupt VRD officials to pocket hard-earned money (NAS, ML 1927, LM 272/47, 28.05.1947; NAS, A000669/16, reel 13; Nanyang Daxue Lishi Xi 1971:50). In another letter, this time addressed to the Chinese Affairs Secretariat, the SRTWU argued that arm badges remained unacceptable to the union. It noted that anyone could find a lost arm badge, wear it, pedal a trishaw and commit an offence. Not surprisingly, the union did not elaborate on how this was possible. The union also felt that it was degrading for the trishaw riders to wear arm badges. No explanation was given for this feeling of degradation but the trishaw riders did not like to ply the streets of Singapore with numbers on their arms displayed prominently. In response, the Municipal Commission argued that there was 'nothing derogatory about an arm badge'. Trishaw riders would be identified by the arm badge number, especially in cases where the passengers were unable to communicate with the riders (*The Straits Times*, 31.05.1947). No agreement was reached on this issue in a meeting between four SRTWU representatives and the Municipal Commission on 17 July 1947. But the SRTWU promised to seriously consider Commissioner Yap Pheng Geck's proposal that the arm badge be replaced by one located on the rider's breast. However, they wanted any such badges to be distributed by the union and demanded that fees for the badges be reduced (*Nanyang Siang Pau*, 18.07.1947; *Sin Chew Jit Poh*, 18.07.1947). When the union's proposal was turned down by the commissioners, the SRTWU made plans for a one-day strike on 1 September.

It was at this moment that the Municipal Commission began considering badges pinned to the breast or coat so that there would not be a reason for a strike. On 1 September, the President of the Municipal Commission claimed that the trishaw riders did not mind wearing badges on their breast or arm (NAS, ML 1927, LM 272/47, 30.08.1947 & 01.09.1947). This change of heart may have led to the SRTWU calling off the strike. Instead, it planned to send six representatives to the Governor for a special meeting. At the meeting held on 11 September, the SRTWU representatives came up with five further proposals, including reduction of trishaw inspections from four annually to three, and for the union to distribute badges and conduct licensing tests. After the meeting, it was publicly announced that arm badges would be replaced by badges on their chests, while it was left to the union to reach a settlement with the VRD over the fine details. Significantly, the union had accepted the Governor's advice not to strike and consequently had obtained the right to conduct licensing tests (*Nanyang Siang Pau*, 01.09.1947; *Sin Chew Jit Poh*, 01.09.1947; *Nanyang Siang Pau*, 12.09.1947; *Sin Chew Jit Poh*, 12.09.1947; NAS, ML 1927, LM 272/47, 12.09.1947).

The threatened strike was one time when Singapore trishaw riders actually flexed their muscles; they had achieved this success only because they had the numbers and were still indispensable to Singapore's transport scene. However, from the late 1940s, the Municipal Commission and its successor the City Council proceeded to place ever increasing limits on the number of trishaws and riders on the streets, as well as prohibiting trishaws from entering certain main streets and thoroughfares. The standard excuse for trying to curtail the number of trishaws was that they were either too slow or took up valuable parking space, implying of course that the vehicles were a traffic hazard. These were the same reasons for calls to ban the trishaws in Ujung Pandang and Yogyakarta. (Forbes 1979:156; Kartodirdjo 1981:36). William Lim had cogently argued that the excuses used to ban trishaws were 'to project a facade of modernisation' (Lim 1975:130). In 1949, due to a reduction in the number of trishaws from the previous year, 'it would appear that trisha riding is not quite as popular as a means of earning a living as it was'. Also that year, in response to such official attitudes and the 'slowness of [the trishaw] overtaking other traffic, and the rapidity with which it can change its direction to either right or left, coupled with the irresponsibility of the riders', it was proposed that parking of *all* vehicles be prohibited in ten roads from 8 a.m. to 6 p.m. and that trishaws be banned totally within three years (Colony of Singapore 1949:7–9).[13]

An effort was also made to introduce motor trishaws but it was not approved by the VRD (SSAR, 'Report of Vehicles Registration Department 1949':30; SSAR, 'Report of Vehicles Registration Department 1950':33; SSAR, 'Report of Vehicles Registration Department 1951':5). In August 1950, George Lee Motors Company applied for permission to sell Czech-made motor trishaws at S$1,825 each. Several tests were conducted in August and September, but the Municipal Commission did not pursue the matter further (*The Straits Times*, 13.09.1950 and 13.11.1950). The Commission had received applications for motor trishaws from George Lee Motors, the STOA and TIPMAS but faced objections to the registration and licensing of these vehicles from the SHTRA (*The Straits Times*, 25.08.1950; MMC, Minutes

---

[13] The ten roads were Stamford Road, South Bridge Road, High Street, Tanjong Pagar Road, New Bridge Road, Orchard Road, North Bridge Road (up to Jalan Sultan), Robinson Road, Victoria Street and Beach Road (between Rochore Road and Jalan Sultan).

of Meeting of Committee No. 1, 01.09.1950; MMC, Minutes of Meeting of Committee No. 1, 02.10.1950). It was likely that the Commission heeded calls from several sectors of the Chinese community who saw the presence of motor trishaws as a threat to the livelihood of the trishaw riders. Even the SCCC and the Singapore Traffic Advisory Committee opposed the introduction of motor trishaws (*Sin Chew Jit Poh*, 05.10.1950; *The Straits Times*, 11.11.1950).

The Municipal Commission continued annually to reduce the number of trishaws and riders. In June 1950 the STOA and TIPMAS themselves called for a reduction in the number of trishaws plying the streets, as both associations found that there were more trishaws than trishaw riders. The associations had to remove all surplus trishaws and so they called for the number of trishaws to be reduced from 7,900 to 5,580 but retaining the ceiling of 9,000 (*The Straits Times*, 29.06.1950). In 1951, the trishaw owners co-operated with the Commission and reduced the number of trishaws from 7,343 to 6,493 after it was declared that the maximum number of riders allowed was 9,000 (*The Singapore Tiger Standard*, 24.01.1951). Furthermore, the following year it was stated that the number of trishaws and riders would be reduced to 6,100 and 6,800 respectively. By 1954, the Commission had further amended that figure, and now the maximum number of trishaws and riders was 4,820 and 5,175 respectively (CSGGS, S82, 31.01.1952; CSGGS, S66, 29.01.1954). On 14 February 1952, the Commission prohibited trishaws from entering Anderson Bridge because they 'are not only a danger to other vehicles but also to themselves'. This was in addition to being already prohibited from entering Beach Road, Connaught Drive and Fullerton Road (NAS, NA 461, MPCCS, Minutes of Meeting of the Vehicles and Traffic Committee, 14.01.1952:1).

In a City Council meeting on 31 August 1955, Councillor SHD Elias moved a motion to ban trishaws. He argued that 'this is an undesirable form of transport which should be eliminated as soon as possible'. Another councillor, AP Rajah, however, opposed the motion, stating that trishaws 'constitute a necessary means of transport in Singapore'. Elias's motion was ultimately dismissed (NAS, NA 466, MPCCS, Minutes of an Ordinary Meeting, 31.08.1955:6–7). However, the Master Plan, in which the large-scale development and utilisation of land in Singapore was made public after three years of preparation in 1955, also viewed trishaws with disdain. Initial studies noted that trishaws, 'because of their size, have a greater delaying effect on motor traffic than bicycles'. The final report of the Master Plan stated that 'the slow-moving trisha, whilst supplementing public transport, takes almost as much room as a car, and is a source of delay to speedier traffic' (Colony of Singapore 1955a:101; Colony of Singapore 1955b:39–40). By the time the Master Plan was reviewed in 1965, 1970, 1975 and 1980, no mention of trishaws as a traffic hazard was necessary.

In 1955, the LF had come to power in elections designed for a partially self-governing Singapore. David Marshall became Singapore's first Chief Minister but he resigned in April 1956 after failing to get the British to provide full autonomy to Singapore. Lim Yew Hock then became Chief Minister. By 1956, the Lim Yew Hock government had considered trishaws a major hindrance to 'proper' road transport. An official inquiry into the Singapore public transport system noted that the trishaw was 'a form of transport which is really out of place in fast-moving motor traffic, despite the skill of the riders'. It was stressed that 'one trisha can slow down a complete traffic lane', and the inquiry's conclusions called for further restrictions on the number of available trishaws (Colony of Singapore 1956:92; Nanyang Daxue Lishi Xi 1971:50–51).

Despite 'national' concerns over the transport system in Singapore, transport policies continued to remain the preserve of the City Council. In August 1956, the City Council prohibited the entry of trishaws into some of the more congested streets in Singapore's city centre (*The Straits Times*, 01.09.1956; NAS, NA 468, MPCCS, Ordinary Meeting, 31.08.1956:3). Political events, however, signalled a possible change in the Council's policy towards trishaw riders. In 1957, the PAP captured 13 out of the 32 seats at stake and Ong Eng Guan was appointed the Mayor of Singapore. One change that came with the new elected Council was the reduction of the quarterly trishaw registration fee from $24 to $12 and the trishaw riders' annual license fee from $12 to $6. Inspections of trishaws were also reduced to once every six months (NAS, A000132/05, reel 4).

The Lim government, however, continued to maintain vigilance over the trishaws. Between 1956 and 1959, the VRD and Traffic Police kept a very sharp eye on the industry for any sort of possible infringement of the law. When Tay Quay Muay was caught by Traffic Police during those years, he was fined $3 for wearing black shorts instead of the normal blue uniform. Lu Tian Lee's friend was fined $30 for carrying goods instead of passengers as it was now stipulated that trishaws could only carry two adults or three children (NAS, Transcript of A000739/03:13; NAS, A000669/16, reel 13).

Looking at the annual summary of offences by trishaw riders between 1949 and 1959, there were ten broad categories of offences. The figures for those prosecuted in seven of the categories were noticeably high during the drag-net in 1954 and 1955. Yet interestingly, it was far easier to commit such offences with impunity between 1956 and 1959. This suggests that riders were far more cautious in the years immediately following the crackdown. The only exception was the unrelenting pressure on unlicensed trishaw riders. Between 1957 and 1959 none of those prosecuted for illegal trishaw riding were acquitted.

The City Council was abolished soon after the PAP took office in 1959 because 'in a small city-state like Singapore, there was no practical need for a two-tier government' (Fong 1979:80). From that time on, all local municipal affairs came under the supervision of various government ministries. Lu Tian Lee believed that once the PAP came to power, the vigilant monitoring of riders by the ROV came to an end. Certainly, trishaw riders now faced far less harassment from ROV officials. It also became easier for the SHTRA to deal with the ROV. The Traffic Police tended to 'close one eye' and let the older riders go about their business unscathed. The only fines trishaw riders usually had to pay now was when they accidentally entered lanes from the wrong end. Lu remembered that in order not to pay fines, he now often had to fetch his passengers via the long way round rather than take short cuts, causing some passengers to complain (NAS, A000669/16, reel 13).

The new PAP Government, however, did not intend to maintain the trishaw industry. In December 1960, then Deputy Prime Minister Toh Chin Chye told the ROV that 'it should be our policy to gradually remove trishaws from the local scene' and that 'the best line of action is not to register any more new trishaws or trisha-riders [sic]' (NAS, CI 307, RV 443/5-11, 08.11.1973). The Registrar of Vehicles explained that 'we have not reduced the number of trisha riders as it was thought that with the unemployment now, any means of giving more employment would be in keeping with Government's policy'. He agreed, however, that traffic on the roads would be smoother if the number of trishaws was reduced (NAS, CI 307, RV 443/5-11, 08.11.1973). From 1962, the policy of the ROV had been to renew any trishaw license within three days of expiry or else the license would be cancelled.

In a Cabinet meeting in November 1973, however, Prime Minister Lee Kuan Yew remarked that there were many trishaws outside hotels in the Orchard Road area and he was under the impression that the trishaws were causing traffic congestion (NAS, CI 307, RV 443/5-11, 06.11.1973). In his reply to the Minister for Communications, the Registrar of Vehicles suggested stopping the issue of new trishaw riders' licenses, the invalidation of any trishaw license for owners who did not hold a trishaw rider's license from 31 December 1974, and the creation of a trishaw-free zone in the city area

(NAS, CI 307, RV 443/5-11, 08.11.1973). The Ministry of Communications approved his suggestions and noted that 'should result in the phasing out of trishaws from our roads', although it was cautioned that 'prohibiting them from major roads ... could result in some trisha riders who depend on this trade for their livelihood being deprived of much of their earnings' (NAS, CI 307, RV 443/5-11, 09.11.1973). The Principal Assistant Secretary in the Ministry, however, noted that more than half of the trishaw riders were below 46 years of age. He believed then that, given full employment conditions in Singapore, these riders 'could easily find employment elsewhere should trishas (sic) be phased out' (NAS, CI 307, RV 443/5-11, 27.11.1973). The ultimate intention was to phase out *all* trishaw riders (NAS, CI 307, RV 443/5-11, 14.10.1974).

The suggestion from the ROV eventually became law. In December 1974, the government announced that 'in order to ease traffic congestion during peak hours in the city central area and also with a view to increasing the safety of trishaw riders', trishaws were prohibited from entering 29 major roads in the inner city area between 7.30 and 9.30 am and 4.30 to 7 pm on weekdays and from 7.30 to 9.30 am and 11.30 to 2 pm on Saturdays (ARROV 1974:7).[14] The Chairman of the SHTRA called this 'the start of the end' for the trishaw riders. *The New Nation* wrote that the trishaw riders could now face the first of many restrictive activities 'which will finally drive them off the road' (*The New Nation*, 01.02.1975).

The SHTRA vociferously protested to the ROV since trishaw riders primarily worked in the inner city area. Enforcement of the new rule would deprive many of them of the primary source of their regular income. At an Annual General Meeting of the SHTRA, Vice-President Yang Lai Huat explained that the President of the STOA, Tay Hwan Chong, and himself had visited the ROV but to no avail (NAS, NA 565, Minutes of the 26th Annual General Meeting of the SHTRA, 05.01.1975). In January 1975, the SHTRA President Lim Kim Peow took a negotiating team from the SHTRA and STOA to the ROV with the hope of persuading the ROV to

---

[14] This was the Road Traffic (Public Service Vehicles) (Vocational Licences and Conduct of Drivers, Conductors and Passengers) (Amendment) Rules, 1974. The 29 streets were St. Andrew's Road, Bras Basah Road, Orchard Road, Penang Road, Stamford Road, Clemenceau Avenue, River Valley Road, Coleman Street, Armenian Street, High Street, New Bridge Road, South Bridge Road, Chulia Street, Battery Road, Market Street, Collyer Quay, Shenton Way, Raffles Quay, Robinson Road, Cecil Street, Cross Street, Upper Cross Street, Boon Tat Street, McCallum Street, Hill Street, Victoria Street, North Bridge Road, Connaught Drive and Fullerton Road.

rescind the new regulations (NAS, NA 565, Minutes of the 26th Swearing-In Ceremony of the Executive Committee of the SHTRA, 02.01.1975). However, the STOA and SHTRA were flatly told by the ROV officials that the restrictions 'would not affect' many trishaw riders and that both associations 'should be able to persuade their members to accept the need to improve traffic conditions in the city area' (NAS, CI 307, RV 443/5-11, 29.01.1975). The six representatives from both the SHTRA and STOA left the meeting empty-handed. Despite the major changes in the road transport system and urban planning in Singapore by the mid-1970s, the trishaws still managed to survive because of the strong intervention of the SHTRA. Nevertheless, it was clear to all concerned that the days of the SHTRA and the trishaw industry itself were numbered as Singapore's economy and society moved into the fast lane of the twenty-first century.

Perceptions of the industry

This chapter explored the role of the trishaw industry within the wider framework of the Singapore community – the services the riders provided; the people who used the trishaws; where the riders usually worked; public perception of the industry; and the role of local and state governments to marginalise the industry. In spite of the trishaws providing a personalised service to passengers, it was clear that not everyone in Singapore saw them in a positive light. Like the rickshaws that were eventually banned in 1947, the trishaws were considered slow and responsible for vehicle accidents on the roads. These were the same reasons given by the various authorities in Southeast Asia to either reduce the number of trishaws or ban them completely. The attempts by the LF and the PAP governments in Singapore after 1955 attest to what I had mentioned in Chapter One about the need for cities in newly emerging nations to look and feel 'modern'. The presence of trishaws and anything from the colonial era such as old shophouses and the trading activities along the Singapore River was seen as a major stumbling block to social and economic progress.

The control of the trishaw industry could be seen in two phases. The first was from the end of the BMA in 1946 to the defeat of the LF government in 1959. During this period, the VRD, Municipal Commission and the LF government made very clear gestures that they intended to reduce the dependency of trishaws as a mode of public transport by issuing a limited number of licences per year, registration of new trishaws, periodic testing of the vehicles to test their roadworthiness, introduction of numbered arm badges and introducing up to ten broad categories of offences for the arrest and prosecution of the riders. It was also in this period that the Master Plan was introduced to the public and there were increasing calls for trishaws to be banned as an 'undesirable' form of transport. The second period from 1959 to 1983 was one where changes were made to the human landscape in Singapore according to the Master Plan. The trishaw industry became increasingly sidelined through an unwritten policy of benign neglect. The city planners and administrators simply left the trishaw industry alone to die a natural death in their belief that people would eventually reject the trishaws for faster motorised transport.

Trishaw riders were also viewed suspiciously by members of the public for their alleged association with secret societies and criminal activities. In time, even trishaw riding was seen to be degrading work carried out by 'beasts of burden'. Trishaw riding came to be regarded as exploitative and disrespectful. However, the trishaw riders knew how to attempt and force people to examine themselves and their impressions of the industry. The riders participated in the charity rides for Nanyang University in 1954, the NDF in 1968 and a new hospital for Chung Hwa Free Clinic in 1972. By announcing their participation in these charity rides, the trishaw riders had effectively shown that they too could exhibit strong support and enthusiasm for the beneficiaries. If people from the lower echelons of society, such as the trishaw riders, could come together for a worthy cause and donate the day's wages to charity, should not the rest of society do the same? No wonder, then, that even today people remember how the trishaw riders had participated in the charity ride for Nanyang University. The next chapter will deal specifically with the extraordinary changes in Singapore's landscape and road transport scene since 1965 and their social and economic repercussions on the trishaw industry.

Chapter 5

THE TWILIGHT YEARS

Independence

The year 1965 marked the advent of a new era in Singapore's history. Politically, colonialism and foreign domination came to an end as Singapore strove to survive on its own after two turbulent years as part of Malaysia. Socially, subsequent years saw escalation of the public housing programme instituted by the PAP Government in 1960 with the founding of the HDB. While economically, the government concentrated its energies on industrialisation and reduction of unemployment by creating new industrial estates at Kallang, Tanjong Rhu, Redhill and Tiong Bahru in addition to Jurong Industrial Estate which was developed in 1961.

However, for those involved in the trishaw industry, the years after 1965 heralded the beginning of the end of their profession and way of life. In fact, the initial decline of the industry can be considered to have been begun from the mid-1950s. From 1954 onwards, the bicycle industry was in decline, which indirectly affected the trishaw industry since fewer trishaws were manufactured. However, both the number of trishaws and riders declined after 1952. These trends coincided with a rise in the number of public buses and taxis, especially after 1955. The years since 1965 also have marked the depopulation of traditional areas of business such as Chinatown and Little India. By the 1970s, Singapore began to position itself as a 'Global City' with the world, rather than Malaya, as its hinterland for trade and communications (Rajaratnam 1987:223–231). If Singapore were to be an 'archetypal world city' (Newman & Thornley 2005:246–254), changes in the land transport system, urbanisation of areas outside the inner city and population shifts had to be enforced. These policies led to the gradual demise of the trishaw industry.

THE TWILIGHT YEARS

Changes in the transport system

Trishaws played a dominant role in Singapore's land transport system in the years immediately following the Japanese Occupation. At that time, public transport had all but collapsed, since 'the lorries, taxis and buses were old and decrepit after years of use and misuse, and breakdowns were the rule rather than the exception' (Ho 1975:186–187). The buses in Singapore were run by the STC, managed by British colonial authorities and which monopolised main roads leading into the inner city, and 11 privately owned Chinese bus companies.[1] There were few taxis plying the roads. At this stage, trishaws still dominated the local transport scene as their numbers far outstripped those of the public buses and taxis combined. Spencer noted then that 'trishaws had the great virtue of being able to run even when motor fuel was unobtainable, and could easily be built by local mechanics using standard bicycle parts' (Spencer 1989:203).

In addition to not being always accessible, problems with the bus services till the late 1960s were further compounded by the fact that each company served only a particular zone, which meant commuters had to switch to different buses as they travelled from place to place. The licence policy of the colonial authorities favoured the STC and the rest of the competitors had to make detours to avoid moving along roads served by the STC (Spencer 1988: 1031–1032; Spencer 1989: 199; Eio 1979:83; Sim 1975:22; Seah 1985:267). Under such circumstances, bus services were 'far from satisfactory' (Seah 1985:268). However, despite the poor bus service, all major companies began to increase their fleet size. The largest private bus company, Tay Koh Yat, for instance, increased its fleet from 58 buses in 1949 to 111 in 1955. By the time the public bus service was reorganised in 1970, Tay Koh Yat had 222 buses (ARMCS 1949; ARVRD 1955; ARVRD 1970).

The pattern of growth in the number of taxis was also phenomenal. In 1949, there were just 1,081 taxis in Singapore; by 1970, there were 3,784 taxis (ARMCS 1949; ARVRD 1970). On top of this three-fold increase, there were also many 'pirate' taxis operating throughout the island, which peaked in 1968 at 1,222 vehicles (Rimmer 1986:125).[2] These 'pirate' vehicles

---

1   2 The 11 Chinese bus companies were Green Bus, Tay Koh Yat Bus, Soon Lee Bus, Ngo Hock Bus, Changi Bus, Keppel Bus, Katong Bedok Bus, Ponggol Bus, Kampong Bahru Bus, Easy Bus and Paya Lebar Bus. In 1951, Soon Lee and Ngo Hock Bus Companies merged to form the Hock Lee Amalgamated Bus Co. These companies operated until 1970.

2   The 'pirate' taxi drivers were a force to be reckoned with, as they went on a two-day strike in March 1966 when the PAP government appeared ready to clamp down on the 'pirate' taxis.

ran on diesel fuel and were not registered with the any authorities. They first appeared in 1950 when the Municipal Council imposed a limit on the number of licensed taxis (Spencer 1988:1031). These 'pirate' vehicles offered the same door-to-door service as the trishaws, and often competed effectively with the bus companies.

As the general population came to repudiate trishaws in favour of motorised public transport, many riders quit the industry because of falling incomes. In December 1960 alone, 464 riders left the profession (*Singapore Free Press*, 16.12.1960). Chua Ah Tong, President of the SHTRA between 1961 and 1968, disappointingly admitted that 'every year we lose about 30 to 40 members' due to old age, ill health or poor earnings (*Malay Mail*, 09.01.1967). Hence, the combined competition from buses, taxis and 'pirate' vehicles ensured that 'the days of profitable trisha-pedalling are numbered' (*Singapore Free Press*, 17.08.1961).

The Government took steps to solve the transport problems only in the 1970s after it had successfully tackled unemployment and housing in the previous decade (Chang 1973:97–100). The Ministry of Communications was formed in 1968 to tackle transport problems including an inefficient public transport service, lack of parking spaces and congestion in the city centre (Chin 1998:83). The modernisation of the public transport system was the death knell for the trishaw industry. There was an inherent belief that 'the future of civilisation lies within the cities and to realise these potentials it is essential to provide improved means of transport within and between these cities' (Yee 1973:54). The 1970s brought major changes to the local transport scene. In 1970, the ten Chinese bus companies merged to form three new corporate companies.[3] These three companies, however, were still internally divided by loyalties to families that previously owned the ten companies. In 1971, the STC collapsed in bankruptcy and its buses were parcelled out among the three companies. In that year too, the government organised a crackdown on 'pirate' taxis by means of a heavy diesel tax, suspension of licence and seizure of vehicles, with the result that many 'pirate' operators were forced to become either bus or taxi drivers (Rimmer 1986:123). Then, in 1973, the three companies were once again amalgamated to form the Singapore Bus Service (SBS). The increased use of buses was in response to the need for an improvement in public transport because buses could provide 'an almost door-to-door service' (Yee 1973:60). By 1980, there was even a

---

[3] These were the Amalgamated Bus Company Ltd., Associated Bus Services Pte. Ltd. and the United Bus Company Pte. Ltd.

debate between those who supported a Mass Rapid Transit (MRT) system and those who felt an all-bus public transport system was good enough (Lim 1975:107–128; Lim 1980:47–52; MRT Review Team 1980; Provisional Mass Rapid Transit Authority 1981). The trishaws were effectively marginalised.

The ROV have retained records of accidents involving trishaw riders between 1959 and 1972. There were fewer accidents involving trishaws as the years went by – not because riders were more traffic conscious but probably because there were fewer trishaws on Singapore's roads. The fall in trishaw numbers resulted in a decline in accidents involving public transport. Nevertheless, the increase in motorised traffic had, by the early 1980s, still resulted in the average death of two cyclists and/or trishaw riders per month. A further three trishaw riders were also injured on average from traffic accidents each month. It was alleged that many riders 'cut' lanes (*The Straits Times*, 09.08.1982).

The great strides in motorised transport went hand-in-hand with the decline of the bicycle industry as well (Nanyang Daxue Lishi Zi 1971:42–45; Yan 1957:preface). The bicycle industry peaked during the period from 1948 to the end of the Korean War in 1953. The trade figures between 1951 and 1953 were the highest, with 1952 being the peak year with 288,014 imported and 170,715 exported. Exports, however, fell sharply in 1953 with the end of the Korean War. When the Korean War broke out, bicycle production temporarily halted in Europe, causing an economic boom for bicycle traders with sudden increased local market demand. As Namazie recalled, 'If there are tensions, well, the benefit comes here' (NAS, Transcript of A000189/11:86). These local traders made over 100 per cent profit on bicycle manufacture and sales but unfortunately did not expand their businesses. When the market started showing signs of stagnating, these traders (mostly Henghuas) slashed the prices of bicycles in order to survive. In the aftermath of the Korean War, Singapore's main export partner Indonesia also faced political instability and their import regulations were not properly enforced. Soon, Singapore traders found the supply of their bicycles far exceeded demand in the region. In desperation, these traders then dumped their bicycles on the Malayan market. However, Malaya had been importing bicycles directly from Europe and Japan and this act of dumping only resulted in a price war and further costs of all bicycles in the country. This unprecedented set of local-regional circumstances caused the decline of the Singapore bicycle industry, from which it never recovered.

Nevertheless, in 1967, the first bicycle factory – the Malaysian United Industries (MUI) Pte. Ltd. – was established at Jurong Industrial Estate with $5 million as capital. But its history was short-lived. On 23 April 1971, due to a lack of sales and an effective marketing strategy, the MUI stopped manufacture and switched to producing watches. All such bicycle factories were in reality nothing more than assembling plants. The PAP government taxed all bicycle spare parts and placed a quota on the number of imported bicycles. Therefore prices of bicycles soared, placing a heavy burden on the consumer. Moreover, the local bicycle factories failed to increase their exports. The market therefore remained small and Singapore could not compete with the reliable foreign bicycles mass produced in China, Japan and Taiwan. The cost of production was higher in Singapore. Added on to the cost too was the fact that all bicycle parts were imported for assembling and taxed at the rate of 40 per cent although the bicycle itself was not taxed. Thus, the local bicycle industry simply could not compete with foreign imports and declined.

This demise affected the trishaw industry as it meant that trishaw owners manufactured fewer trishaws than before. The promotion of bus and taxi services at the expense of the trishaw by the PAP Government also played a significant part since such a campaign helped erase the 'undeveloped' image of the city. The government embraced Western urban technology and planning in the belief that this was most desirable and employed Australian consulting firm Crooks Michell Peacock Stewart to help shape Singapore's future landscape. Dick and Rimmer considered such consultation to be part of a process of 'imperialism of urban public transport' since the consultants and their overseas-trained local planners excluded trishaws from their development projects. Indeed, their 1971 report called for the development of an MRT system within two decades (Rimmer 1986:124; Dick & Rimmer 1986:184–185). Such large scale ambitious goals compelled trishaws to 'wither away' (Rimmer 1988:792).

Urbanisation and its effects

Another major cause of the decline of the trishaw industry was the development of new outlying areas – suburbs – which depopulated parts of the older inner city core. Prior to such initiatives in the early 1960s, urban Singapore under colonial rule was supposedly still 'unique' in that 'it captures the mysterious and exotic Orient' which tourists and other travellers flocked to experience at first-hand (Savage 1992a:13). There was 'a rhythm of energy, vibrancy and impatience' because of the constant movement of people, goods and vehicles (Savage 1992a:15). Ommanney likened the economic life of the city to that of an urban jungle where 'survival is to the fittest' and so 'many climb over their prostrate competitors and reach the daylight above' (Ommanney 1960:35–36). Moore, however, noted that nothing in Singapore was permanent (Moore 1955:64); and the urban development of Singapore destroyed much of the old hustle and bustle of Singapore, and it forced trishaw riders to move out of the inner city to seek customers elsewhere.

The purpose of the new massive urbanisation programme was twofold: one was to move population from 'decaying' inner city areas to 'New Towns' in outlying districts, while the other was to eradicate all the slums and squatters' settlements in the heart of the inner city (Savage 1992b:17). The goal of removing long-standing residents from the inner city, especially Chinatown, ensured that Singapore would be transformed into a centre for business and trans-national capital rather than remain largely a residential area (Eio 1979:85). The inner city had to be transformed because of severe overcrowding that was made even more acute by the post-war baby boom (Grice & Drakakis-Smith 1985:351; McGee 1967:155). The construction of Queenstown, an estate of about 526 acres, began in 1952 but completed by 1969. This was followed by a 600-acre new town at Toa Payoh, which was ready by 1973 (Housing & Development Board 1970:21 & 26). The HDB then moved to also provide housing blocks at Bedok and Telok Blangah in the early 1970s. The Singapore Improvement Trust (SIT) – predecessor of the HDB – was meant to have built low-cost housing according to a 1955 Master Plan to encourage people to leave the inner city. The Master Plan envisaged satellite towns ringing the inner city with a 'green belt' formed as a dividing barrier between the two. But the overall SIT housing programme was woefully inadequate – in its 32 years of operations, it built only 23,300 housing units. The HDB, on the other hand, provided 32,000 flats and shop units alone between 1960 and 1963. In 1965, a Concept Plan was formulated in which housing estates were planned and linked with improved roads, expressways and even a mass rapid rail system (Seah 1985:262–263). It was clear that 'land-use decisions by public agencies are changing the entire face of Singapore island and affecting Singapore's way of life' (Gamer 1972:131).

Extraordinary change in Singapore's demography was also evident. Between 1957 and 1970, for example, Queenstown experienced a 1,806 per cent increase in population with 99 per cent of the residents of this new town living in HDB flats. Correspondingly, Kreta Ayer (which includes

Chinatown) witnessed a 39 per cent fall in population, while only 16 per cent lived in HDB accommodation. Tan notes that these population shifts were 'clearly tied up with the various public-sector programmes of development in housing, urban renewal and industry' (Tan 1975:57). It is estimated that in the years between 1960 and 1965, about 400,000 people came to live in HDB flats (Li 1968:64).

The new housing estates were also used to resettle people who used to live in slums and squatters' settlements, and even kampongs disappeared as the years progressed. By 1965, there was real recognition that the inner city had to be totally cleared of the 'shabbiness of the flimsy, miserable huts of the squatter colonies and the overcrowded noise tenements' (McGee 1967:155). New roads were created for the developing outlying towns as well. During this rapid urbanisation process, many old roads also disappeared. Thus, places such as Anguilla Road, Muar Road and Park Road have vanished. Johore Road is now virtually an empty street with no shophouses in sight. Naturally, these developments affected trishaw riders directly as it meant loss of their own homes and right of way to ply for hire. The new estates were self-contained often employing population in places within or nearby the housing developments. By 1971, for instance, there were 284 factories in Jurong employing 35,000 people. A quarter of all workers in Jurong lived there (Owen 1972:70–76). This wholesale destruction of slums, squatters' settlements and villages meant loss of considerable income for trishaw riders as their clientele were removed from the traditional inner urban areas. Today, many of these riders, now elderly men, can be seen plying the streets of the housing estates nearest the city in search of customers such as Geylang, Marine Parade and Katong.

The net result of urbanisation was the moving away of the population from the city centre into the outlying areas, where new housing estates were built. This had an impact on the trishaw industry. Before urbanisation, the population were cramped in shophouses and quarters in the city centre. It made sense to either walk or take a trishaw because the distance travelled was short. The Australian consulting firm of Crooks Michell Peacock Stewart found that in 1971, two-fifths of the population lived and worked in shophouses and they walked, cycled or took a trishaw to work (Rimmer and Dick 2009:57). Buses were used when one wanted to travel out of the city. With urbanisation, however, the population moved out of the city centre. The trishaw riders were still living in their old quarters and the movement of people made it harder for them – especially as they aged – to travel further and further out of the city.

Ironically, the passing of pre-war Singapore has led nowadays to calls for conservation of urban historical areas such as Chinatown and Little India. These were precisely the traditional areas which suffered major loss of population and relocation – for example, in Chinatown, population density had dropped by 50 per cent in the early 1960s as people moved out (Gopalakrishnan & Perera 1983:47). However, these conservation efforts only took off in 1986, long after the trishaw industry collapsed. Furthermore, the Potemkin-like facade and daily life of the new Chinatown was vastly different from what it once was like. In the case of Tanjong Pagar, for instance, conservation 'has erased the former economic landscape dominated by the small family business' which had been of immense benefit to the trishaw industry in that locale. Instead, the new Tanjong Pagar is 'specialised, modern and upmarket', which has left the area largely bereft of people and quiet during the day (Yeoh & Lau 1995:54).

Advent of the tourist boom

In the 1960s and 1970s, as parts of old Singapore were demolished in favour of new buildings, a movement began to preserve Singapore's urban heritage (Tyner 2003:485). In November 1965, the Singapore Tourist Promotion Board (STPB) laid plans to construct several trishaw stands in the city area. Its Chairman, K M Byrne, visited the Cathay Hotel, Goodwood Hotel and Hotel Singapura to choose appropriate sites for these stands. The STPB had considered trishaws to be 'great tourist attractions' (*The Straits Times*, 03.11.1965). The tourist agencies were seen to be the saviour of the trishaw industry (*The Straits Times*, 26.10.1971). The Registrar of Vehicles, in his letter to the Minister for Communications, remarked that perhaps the Prime Minister had seen so many trishaws in the Orchard Road area as a consequence of these trishaw stands (NAS, CI 307, RV 443/5-11, 08.11.1973). Attempts were made to promote Singapore as a tourist destination. New tourist attractions such as the Jurong Bird Park and the Singapore Zoological Gardens were opened. Even then, it had been remarked that the new attractions might not 'overcome the disability of a city that is not itself interesting' (Gamer 1972:135). Strangely, the trishaws were to eventually find a new lease of life as part of the tourist industry. In July 1972, fifty undergraduates from the University of Singapore participated in a trishaw pageant that proceeded from the campus at Bukit Timah towards Orchard Road. The 25 pairs of riders and passengers used decorated trishaws hired from the SHTRA (*The Straits Times*, 14.07.1972). Later that year, when Humphrey B Bear, a character from an Australian children's television programme, visited Singapore, he was taken on a ride along the Singapore River in a trishaw (*The Straits Times*, 22.11.1972).

By 1973, as the Ministry of Communications began a gradual phasing out of trishaws in Singapore, the STPB intervened in a bid to save the industry, albeit for tourism. In its appeal to the Permanent Secretary in the Ministry, the STPB wrote that trishaw riders should not be deprived of their livelihood. Furthermore, the STPB believed that 'trishas and trisha (sic) riders are one element which helps to create an atmosphere of Singapore as an exotic, eastern city' (NAS, CI 307, RV 443/5-11, 19.11.1973). The STPB then conducted a survey on tourist demand for trishaws in April 1974. The board found that most of the tourists who took the trishaws on these 'trishaw tours' organised by 11 tourist agencies were Americans and Australians. It concluded that 105 trishaws would be enough for the tourism industry for the period 1974 to 1977 (NAS, CI 307, RV 443/5-11, April 1974).

The Ministry of Communications did not share the enthusiasm of the STPB. An official noted on a letter from the STPB that 'this Ministry does *not* recognise that trishaws have a touristic appeal' (NAS, CI 307, RV 443/5-11, 19.10.1974).[4] The STPB, however, would organise a pool of trishaws to operate from several hotels in order to ensure 'safe modus operandi for tourists' (NAS, CI 307, RV 443/5-11, 02.11.1974). The STPB proceeded to employ young healthy men who could speak English for its pool of trishaw riders. In early 1975, the STPB laid down plans to deploy 200 'attractive and well maintained trishaws' at ten selected hotels. The riders had to be between 30 to 45 years of age who would be provided with 'attractive uniforms to create an oriental flavour' (NAS, CI 307, RV 443/5-11, 05.02.1975). In September 1976, the STPB distributed survey forms to 476 trishaw riders. Out of the 112 who replied, however, the STPB found that only 41 of them were below 40 years of age and could speak English. The STPB also had to conduct interviews with these 41 trishaw riders in February (NAS, CI 307, RV 443/5-11 Vol 2, 05.01.1977).

From providing a means of transport for local people, trishaw riding was now seen to have a significant role in the booming tourist industry. In its report on tourists taking trishaw rides in Chinatown, *The New Nation* noted that 'trishaws are saved from extinction by tourists who are thrilled by such rides' (*The New Nation*, 13.03.1975). The advent of the tourist boom

---

[4] Emphasis in original.

in Singapore from the late 1970s, therefore, had given trishaw riding a 'shot in the arm' (*The Straits Times*, 16.10.1978). Trishaw Tours was founded in 1978 to organise trishaw rides for tourists. The STPB also had to look into any instances of irregularities committed by travel agents (*The Straits Times*, 04.10.1978 and 07.10.1978). The new trishaw riders were usually part-time workers who took up riding to supplement their income. They were often younger, and picked up tourists only. The fares now charged, however, were exorbitant compared with what the older riders charged. In 1978, an hour's ride covering Orchard Road and Shenton Way according to the Municipal rate cost $1.50 while these young part-timers were charging ten dollars (*The Straits Times*, 29.05.1978). In 1980, there were European tourists who would even purchase a whole trishaw and ship it home (*The New Nation*, 29.04.1980).

However, this new boost for a dying industry soon got out of hand. By 1981, there were regular reports in the newspapers of trishaw riders harassing tourists. The ROV and police were called in after tourists complained of being hustled by some riders who had demanded as much as US$200 'after taking their passengers to a dark spot' (*The Straits Times*, 09.12.1981). A few Venezuelan and Japanese tourists also complained about how they were overcharged by two trishaw riders. Two suspects in each case were rounded up after Interpol intervened (*The Straits Times*, 22.12.1981 and 22.09.1982).

By 1982, history had come full circle as steps were taken once again to regulate the trishaw industry. Only riders registered with three trishaw companies – Heritage Tours, Associated Tours and Trishaw Tours – could pick up and drop tourists at certain points. Trishaws meant for tourists were now painted a different colour, and riders had to wear identification tags and prominently display the name of companies who employed them. The ROV also stepped up patrols so as to ensure no further harassment of tourists. And finally, a register of all trishaw riders was kept with the ROV to help regulate trishaw tours in the inner city (*The Straits Times*, 03.08.1982 and 21.09.1982). A new trishaw ride was also launched as part of 'The Singapore Experience' in September 1982, although it got off to a dismal start when only six passengers out of 25 turned out to be tourists. The rest were staff of the trishaw companies or their friends (*The Straits Times*, 22.09.1982). To appeal to tourists further, the riders began installing radios in their trishaws. The ROV declared since trishaws were 'public service vehicles', they would need its approval before radios could be installed.

Trishaw tours, however, still continued despite problems faced by the ROV. These tours were regarded as a form of live (albeit 'exotic') entertainment, and a cultural-historical attraction. Trishaw cavalcades were led by a guide who provided commentaries on tourist attractions on the island (Teo 1982:34 & 171). However, these guides were often nothing more than 'culture brokers', as they only pointed out things that fascinated tourists and fulfilled their desire to capture the authentic (Cohen, Nir & Almagor 1992:225–226). Usually tourists would be cycled to historical areas such as Chinatown and Little India. Such tours gave tourists and other visitors a feel for the 'Asian experience', a chance to quite literally plough through 'instant Asia' (Spencer 1989:203; Grice & Drakakis-Smith 1985:348). The trishaw had become a powerful symbol and metaphor on the island of the 'exotic' East with teeming populations and man-powered labour.

The collapse of the trishaw industry

Despite the boost to the industry provided by the tourist boom, the late 1970s marked the death knell of the formal trishaw industry. The end of the industry came just as suddenly as its advent during the Japanese Occupation. In a way, the three trishaw organisations traced in this book succumbed to the inevitable. The first organisation that was directly affected by drastic changes to the transport system and urban landscape was the STOA. At its peak in 1960, the STOA claimed 423 members according to the ROS; by the time of its final Annual General Meeting (AGM) in January 1977, there were only 30 owners left (NAS, MHA 445, R of S 181/47, 31.05.1960 & Annual Returns of the STOA 1977).

On 8 December 1977, the President of the STOA, Tay Kim Geok, wrote of the inevitable decline to the ROS: 'We regret to say that the members were getting less and less and so is the said trishaw vehicles' (NAS, MHA 445, R of S 181/47, 08.12.1977). Considering that the membership of the organisation had markedly dwindled, the STOA decided to dissolve itself. On 8 March 1978, a general meeting of the remaining 20 members of the STOA was convened and 16 voted for dissolution. The remaining STOA funds of $134.20 were spent to cover rent due on the association's premises at 84-A Bencoolen Street (NAS, MHA 445, R of S 181/47, Certificate of Dissolution). On 16 March, the STOA was declared dissolved.

The SHTRA also faced declining membership as a result of illness and death or members returning to China. Out of 228 members on the roll between 1971 and 1976, 18 died during this period and three returned to China (NAS, NA 565, SHTRA, Monthly Subscription Record Book,

1971–1976). The SHTRA also faced the additional problem of leadership succession. On 30 January 1972, Chan Boon Tong was elected Assistant Auditor of the SHTRA but he died in June. His successor, Hong Kim Chwee, also died in October. The SHTRA then persuaded the Assistant Treasurer, Lim Kim Peow, to take the appointment until the next AGM (NAS, NA 565, SHTRA, Minutes of the 5th meeting of the 23rd Executive Committee, 08.10.1972). Throughout the 1970s, the same individuals in the SHTRA were elected again and again to various positions in the association. The lack of new blood was evident at the 25th AGM of the SHTRA in 1974, when the secretary, Teng Ah Twee, urged remaining SHTRA members to encourage other riders to join the association as it had been reduced to 159 members (NAS, NA 565, SHTRA, Minutes of the 25th AGM, 06.01.1974). The declining membership meant the association had virtually lost what little political power it still had as its members unsuccessfully petitioned the government to lift the ban on entry to 29 inner city roads. It appeared too that many trishaw riders simply left the association so as not to pay the monthly subscription fee (Nanyang Daxue Lishi Xi 1971:51). Ng Kah Eng, treasurer during the last years of the SHTRA, was bitterly disappointed younger riders did not bother to join the association, due to the excuse that the latter, as independents, could earn just as much money as the older trishaw riders. Therefore, the subscription fee was considered to be a waste of money (NAS, Transcript of A000117/09:78). This rejection of the union and its principles by his younger colleagues was to have grave consequences for the association.

By May 1980, it was reported that no new members had joined the SHTRA and its mutual aid branch, the SHTRMBO. On 25 November, the President, Lim Kim Peow, requested that dissolution forms for the SHTRMBO be mailed to the association (NAS, MSA 2962, RMBO 1.328.2, 01.05.1980 & 25.11.1980). The final straw came with the machinations of the new owner of the association's premises, Tan Hai Chuan, who bought the premises from its previous Japanese owner for $30,000. Ironically, the SHTRA had been offered the premises by the Japanese for only $20,000 in August 1978 (*The Straits Times*, 03.09.1980).[5] Tan and his father-in-law, Tiang Tien Ho, who owned a bar next door, wanted the tenants to move out by June 1979 but the SHTRA refused. The SHTRA circulated a letter which angrily condemned both Tiang and Tan for snatching the premises away from the association by

---

[5] The premises at 40, Bencoolen Street was shared by the SHTRA, the Hsinghai Art Association and a Chinese physician named Koh Tack Yong.

offering $10,000 more (NAS, MSA 2962, RMBO 1.328.2, 08.03.1981). To make matters worse, Tan took the SHTRA to court for illegal occupation of his premise and the court ruled that the SHTRA and all other occupants had to vacate the building by the end of March 1981. Resigned to their fate, the SHTRA requested that their mutual aid branch be dissolved. They had seemingly decided 'to bite the bullet' (NAS, MSA 2962, RMBO 1.328.2, 04.04.1981). Attempts to find alternative accommodation failed. On 30 March 1981, the SHTRMBO held an AGM to decide its future in which 84 of the 106 members voted for dissolution (NAS, RMBO 1.328.2, 23.07.1981). The SHTRMBO was officially abandoned on 24 July 1981, and the organisation's remaining funds of $2,200 were donated to the Chung Hwa Free Clinic since, in the words of the SHTRA secretary, 'we do not need the money any more' and therefore 'it is only proper to donate it to charity' (*The Straits Times*, 18.11.1981).

However, this did not end the struggle from their standpoint. At an Executive Committee meeting of the SHTRA held on 3 May 1981, the association vowed to continue to fight to keep their original premise. However, at an ensuing meeting, it was announced the government had now taken over the site (NAS, NA 565, SHTRA, Minutes of the 3rd meeting of the 32nd Executive Committee, 03.05.1981 & Minutes of the 4th meeting, 06.09.1981). With only 96 members left paying a subscription fee of 50 cents each, the association could not find anywhere else to rent to carry on its work. The government also stopped collecting the $48 annual licence fees from trishaw owners because the amount collected was not enough to cover administration costs (*The Straits Times*, 17.11.1981). In November 1982, one hundred elderly people from St John's Home for the Aged were taken on a one-kilometre trishaw ride. The report by *The Straits Times* noted that 'it was a fitting way to relive nostalgia for the old folk'. The newspaper also recalled that 'once upon a time', trishaws were 'perhaps the most importance mode of public transport in Singapore' (*The Straits Times*, 29.11.1982). It is clear, therefore, that by 1982, the old trishaw industry was no more.

The end of the old industry came quickly after that. On 31 March 1983, the SHTRA announced that due to the lack of capital to pay up rent due for the premises, the association decided to 'die a natural death'; its remaining $105.59 in the treasury was also donated to the Chung Hwa Free Clinic. The association to its very end could not lure new members to join as younger riders were all 'moonlighting' with no interest in joining the SHTRA (*The Straits Times*, 01.04.1983). The premises were then demolished as part of the government's redevelopment plan. The SHTRA was formally dissolved on

15 April 1983. A newspaper commentator noted that while there were still young trishaw riders around to convey tourists, the 'real' trishaw industry was effectively dead (*Lianhe Zaobao*, 02.04.1983).

Riding into nostalgia

The end of the old Chinese trishaw industry came in 1983 when the trishaw-based associations voluntarily dissolved themselves due to the lack of subscriptions to keep the associations financially alive. While tourism had indeed given trishaw riding 'a shot in the arm', many of the younger riders cycling the vehicles for trishaw companies refused to join the SHTRA simply because the association was seen to be gathering of elderly men. The younger riders did not regard trishaw riding as a long-term occupation — many of them were simply in it because of the money that came from the tourist boom.

The experience of the trishaw riders showed that despite the economic take-off that Singapore enjoyed from independence in 1965, there were groups of people who had become marginalised and there was nowhere else for them to go or new jobs for them to do on account of their age. They were unskilled labourers but trishaw riding was a trade that they had been involved in since the end of World War II. By the 1970s, Singapore had embarked on a journey of urban redevelopment and changes in the transport system (especially the bus services) were introduced. The ban of trishaws on certain streets in the city centre sidelined the riders even further.

Trishaw riding had one disadvantage compared to motorised transport in that there was a limit to how far the rider could cycle before it became too arduous for him to carry on. Trishaw riding was good for short distances such as a ride to the nearby market, to fetch children to school or to go to the neighbouring housing estate. The trishaw riders themselves lived in districts 7 and 8 which were close to the city centre. As Chinatown in the city centre and Little India (close to districts 7 and 8) were increasingly depopulated from the 1970s, the trishaw riders found themselves short of potential passengers. It would be unreasonable to ask a rider to cycle his trishaw all the way from the city centre to the new housing estates of Toa Payoh (central Singapore) and Bedok (eastern Singapore). A bus or taxi ride would be faster and more convenient. Considering the difficulty by the SHTRA in recruiting new members, it would be fair to assume that many trishaw riders simply abandoned the trade and left the association. Those who continued to ply the streets did so because they needed the money to survive. When the Government announced that it was no longer collecting the annual licence fees from trishaw owners, it was the signal that the old Chinese trishaw industry that had served Singapore's transport needs so valiantly from the 1940s had suffered an immense decline. By the time the SHTRA was dissolved in 1983, trishaw riding had either become part of people's memories and nostalgia or had become an integral part of the tourist industry of Singapore. In the former case, people remembered with fondness – and this is evident from the oral history interviews used in this publication – the days when life in Singapore was slower and travelling in a trishaw was common. They failed to see the hardship faced by the trishaw riders in trying to make ends meet. In the latter case, the tourists riding in a trishaw were simply soaking up the 'Asian experience' and the riders involved with the trishaw companies were a totally different group altogether. Today, only a few old men can be seen plying the streets in the city centre.

Conclusion

THE TRISHAW INDUSTRY IN PERSPECTIVE

As early as 1961, Chan Chin Bock – who later became Chairman of the Economic Development Board in Singapore – wrote that 'as surely as the rickshaws of Singapore went off the roads for humane reasons, the trishaws are going for economic ones'. The end of the road for the trishaws seemed so certain because of the increasing numbers of motorised public transport. Chan insisted that 'the riders know it, the owners know it and so does the public' but he conceded that 'until the last half-dozen disappear they'll serve as evidence of a more rigorous past' (Chan 1961:63).

This publication is not in any real sense a political-economic history of post-war Singapore. The author has deliberately avoided discussion of Singapore's turbulent post-war political history, which has characterised many recent historical accounts, except where absolutely necessary. For those involved making their livelihood from the trishaw industry, everyday life often assumed far more significance than major turning points in Singapore's political history. It has steered away from looking at prominent people in the history of Singapore. The trishaw industry remains part of Singapore's past that is now increasingly forgotten as society looks forward. What is a representation of the past is quickly brushed aside in the mad-cap rush towards attaining symbols of economic modernisation and transport efficiency.

This social history of the trishaw industry is instead a modest survey of particular socio-historical and economic relationships within Singapore. It seeks to answer three basic questions. Firstly, what was the relationship between the trishaw industry and the colony and later, the state. Secondly, what was the nature of the relationships within the trishaw industry itself, with particular reference to the riders. Here, the evolution of modern

Singapore is framed through the eyes of the riders. Finally, the position of the trishaw industry within the wider society across time is examined.

Gilderhus has written that 'history no longer sets forth common stories that presumably speak for the identity and experience of all readers' (Gilderhaus 1992:123). In this context, the study of the daily lives and circumstance of ordinary people in Singapore represent a 'new history' or a 'people's history' (Burke 2001:1–24; Rimmer, Manderson & Barlow 1990:3–22; Warren 1986:316–27). This research work has attempted to situate Singapore's recent history within the framework of this new history: the trishaw industry's rise and demise also reflects changes in the social fabric of Singapore society since 1945. The industry began during the Japanese Occupation although earlier unsuccessful attempts had been made to introduce the trishaw. It was a trade dominated by two minor *bang* – the Henghuas and Hokchias. The industry experienced a phenomenal growth with the sudden abolition of rickshaws in 1947, and the still generally poor public transport services available till the mid-1950s. The trishaws were manufactured locally and its design regulated by the Municipal Commission.

There are inextricable links between the history and development of the bicycle and trishaw industries. Trishaws were usually sent to bicycle shops for repairs and maintenance. Many trishaw owners were bicycle shop proprietors as well. The STOA, first registered in 1947 to represent the interests of trishaw owners, ensured that the fledgling industry was regulated properly and that trishaw rents were duly collected. The only times daily rents were waived in the period under investigation was during the charity rides conducted for Nanyang University in 1954 and the NDF in 1968.

The trishaws provided a key form of transport at a time when public transport was inefficient. After the end of World War II, as the British returned and rebuilt the Crown Colony, buses and taxi remained poorly managed and people took the trishaw as a cheap and quick means of getting to their destination. However, as the economy of Singapore began to improve, the trishaw industry came to be increasingly sidelined. Curbs were introduced by the authorities who prohibited trishaws from entering certain streets in downtown Singapore because they were considered slow, and hence, would hog the lanes at drivers' expense. The same argument had been used to ban rickshaws but the trishaws were not banned so long as they continued to provide a means of public transport. An attempt at introducing motor trishaws did not work out, but the trishaw industry continued to suffer negative publicity because of the perception that the trishaw riders were linked with crime and the seedy side of life.

THE TRISHAW INDUSTRY IN PERSPECTIVE

Far more is known about the trishaw riders than the owners. Their relationship with the owners was not cordial during the BMA and in the late 1940s, but both the owners and riders began working together for common good, such as participating in charitable causes. Many of the trishaw riders were migrants from northern Fujian Province, had little or no education, some used to work as rickshaw pullers, and they often lived in decrepit accommodation or slums in the city districts near entertainment areas. They occupied the lower socio-economic strata of society and usually worked long hours. However, until the late 1950s, they earned reasonably good wages compared with other informal sector occupations and manual labour. The SHTRA was founded in 1950 to provide mutual aid and explain government regulations to the riders. Their mutual aid organisation was registered as the SHTRMBO in 1961 at the behest of the RMBO. But the political clout of the SHTRA was generally weak. It eventually experienced a decline in membership from the late 1960s. In a way, the trishaw industry could not escape from the clutches of time. Heavier motor vehicle traffic and systematic depopulation of the inner city area led to the slow but inevitable decline of the industry. When the numbers of trishaws, owners and riders fell to exceptionally low levels in the late 1970s, all three organisations then folded by 1983.

The study of how so-called 'peripheral' traffic (Varaprasad 1989:423) situated on the fringes of society can adapt itself to progressive developmental changes sweeping across a society like Singapore has been the subject of considerable research. For instance, Lee noted that 'the question of transport concerns more than transport: it reveals what officials thought about people, big companies and the idea of modernity' (Lee 1986:15). A prevailing theme in this social history of the trishaw industry is how it failed to adapt to the tremendous economic and environmental changes occurring in post-war Singapore. In the late 1940s, rickshaws were rejected by the public and local government on humanitarian grounds. By the 1960s, as Singapore entered a period of phenomenal economic growth, motorised public transport expanded rapidly and trishaws were now increasingly relegated to the sole role of conveying tourists on city tours.

Lian has argued that 'any social history of the Chinese in Singapore has to take into account the rich literature on the social organisation of the overseas Chinese' (Lian 1992:100). Yet, surprisingly, there are no publications that analyse the social and economic contribution of the Henghuas and Hokchias to Singapore's historical development. Most historical accounts tend to evaluate the economic and political achievements of the dominant

Hokkien dialect group and its commercial and political leaders. Therefore, in this social history, the only way that the author could begin to explore and clarify the accomplishments of these minor dialect groups was to carefully scrutinise the clan associations' souvenir magazines. Unpublished records from both the associations of the trishaw owners and riders have to be used. The oral recordings with retired trishaw riders have a tremendous value when it comes to understanding their lives and challenges.

This publication aims to understand the position of the trishaw industry in a Singapore that was progressing from Crown Colony to nationhood and to situate it within the economic and societal changes taking place. For those involved with the trishaw industry, their lives were never really understood by the Chinese community and public perception began to conjure up images of the riders that were unfair to them.

It is hoped that this study of trishaw owners and riders, particularly the latter, will shed light on the daily lives and historical circumstance of those Henghuas and Hokchias involved in a 'dying trade'. Their occupation and experiences can also be considered in the context of other historical studies of prominent Singaporeans as well as the wider history of post-war Singapore. It must be emphasised here that social history should review the life and circumstance of those in the upper echelons of society too, while also descending the social ladder to investigate those at the lower end. Social history must attempt to chart the lives of those involved in an industry who would ultimately be 'overwhelmed by the hopelessness and powerlessness of their situation' (Lian 1992:100).

APPENDIX 1

The 'bang'-based trades of Singapore

Dialect Group (% of Chinese in Singapore in the 1980 census)	Predominant Place(s) of Origin	Trades That They Dominated in Singapore
Hokkien (43.1%)	Quanzhou, Zhangzhou, Yongchun and Longyan Prefectures in southern Fujian Province	Nearly all the work available in Singapore from lightboat workers to rich entrepreneurs. Dominant in the rubber and pineapple industries, tugboat trade, banking and finance, import/export trade, shipping industry and the provision shop (retail) business.
Teochew (22.0%)	Chaozhou Prefecture in Guangdong Province except Dabu and Fengshun districts	Dominant in the pineapple industry, fishing industry, trading in market produce, wholesalers and retailers in local produce, and as night-soil collectors, farmers (of poultry, pigs and/or vegetables), goldsmith shop operators, jewellers, and boatmen.
Cantonese (16.5%)	Guangzhou and Zhaoqing Prefectures in Guangdong Province	Dominant among hairdressers, beauticians, mechanics, artisans, goldsmiths, restaurant operators, paper craftsmen, carpenters and construction workers.
Hakka/Kheh (7.4%)	Jiayingzhou Prefecture, the Dabu and Fengshun districts in Chaozhou Prefecture, Huizhou Prefecture (all in Guangdong Province) as well as the Yongding and Shanghang districts in Fujian Province	Dominant among shoe and slipper manufacturers, blacksmiths, Chinese herbal and medicine specialists, textile and garment manufacturers, jewellers and iron foundry workers.
Hainanese (7.1%)	Qiongzhou Prefecture (official name for Hainan Island) in Guangdong Province	Dominant in coffee shop industry and bakeries, as well as houseboys, seamen/sailors, cooks, domestic servants and canteen operators.
Foochow (1.7%)	Fuzhou Prefecture in northern Fujian Province	Dominant in coffee shop, hotel, printing and transport (especially bus) industries, as well as barbers.

Dialect Group (% of Chinese in Singapore in the 1980 census)	Predominant Place(s) of Origin	Trades That They Dominated in Singapore
Henghua (0.7%)	Xinghua Prefecture in northern Fujian Province	Dominant as rickshaw pullers, trishaw riders, taxi drivers as well as controlling the bicycle and automobile spare parts industries. Later shifted to hotel management, real estate management and banking on a small scale.
Hokchia (<1%)	Fuqing district in Fuzhou Prefecture in Fujian Province	Dominant as rickshaw pullers, trishaw riders, and bus operators. Also shared control over the bicycle and automobile spare parts industries. Later shifted to hotel management on a small scale.
Sanjiangren (0.8%)	Outside the provinces of Fujian and Guangdong. Mainly from Jiangxi Province, Jiangsu Province, Shanghai, and the Ningbo and Wenzhou districts of Zhejiang Province	Dominant as laundry shop operators, carpenters, tailors and furniture manufacturers and refurbishers.

Sources: Cheng 1985; Singapore Federation of Chinese Clan Associations 1990; Tan 1990.

APPENDIX 2

Membership and leaders of the Singapore Trishaw Owners' Association, 1946–1978

Year	No. of Members	President	Secretary	Treasurer
1947	40	Not known	Not known	Not known
1948	Not known	Not known	Not known	Not known
1949	285	Not known	Lim Teck Tong	Not known
1950	360	Tay Ah Hong	Lim Teck Tong	Not known
1951	Not known	Tay Ah Hong	Lim Teck Tong	Lim Kow Puay
1952	Not known	Not known	Not known	Not known
1953	120	Ng Ah Pee	Lim Teck Tong	Tan Ah Yong
1954	142	Ng Ah Pee	Lim Teck Tong	Lim Ah Chio
1955	153	Chia Keng Cheng	Lim Teck Tong	Lim Ah Chio
1956	180	Chia Keng Cheng	Lim Teck Tong	Lim Ah Chio
1957	180	Ng Ah Pee	Lim Teck Tong	Lim Khe Ee
1958	176	Ng Ah Pee	Lim Teck Tong	Tan Ah Yong
1959	421	Ng Ah Pee	Lim Teck Tong	Tan Ah Yong
1960	423	Ng Ah Pee	Lim Teck Tong	Tan Ah Yong
1961	51	Ng Ah Pee	Tan Kee Leng	Tay Ah Toh
1962	45	Ng Ah Pee	Tan Kee Leng	Teng Ah Thor
1963	43	Ng Ah Pee	Tan Kee Leng	Teng Ah Thor
1964	45	Tay Hwan Chong	Tay Ah Toh	Teng Ah Thor
1965	35	Tay Hwan Chong	Tan Ah Yong	Teng Ah Thor
1966	45	Tay Hwan Chong	Kuar Ah Boi	Teng Ah Thor
1967	43	Tay Hwan Chong	Kuar Ah Boi	Teng Ah Thor
1968	62	Tay Hwan Chong	Ng Boon Hin	Teng Ah Thor
1969	43	Tay Hwan Chong	Tan Ah Yong	Kuar Ah Boi
1970	42	Tay Hwan Chong	Kuar Ah Boi	Teng Ah Thor
1971	25	Tay Hwan Chong	Teng Ah Thor	Tan Ah Yong
1972	36	Tay Hwan Chong	Kuar Ah Boi	Teng Ah Thor
1973	37	Ng Boon Hin	Tay Ah Toh	Tay Kay Poh
1974	30	Tay Hwan Chong	Tay Kay Poh	Tan Geok Koon
1975	30	Tay Hwan Chong	Kuar Ah Boi	Tay Kay Poh
1976	30	Tay Hwan Chong	Kuar Ah Boi	Tay Kay Poh
1977	30	Tay Kim Geok	Liow Chor Lee	Swee Kim Choo
1978	20	Swee Kim Choo	Tan Geok Koon	Liow Chor Lee

Sources: R of S 181/47, Annual Returns of the STOA, 1953–1978; Annual Report of the Labour Department, Singapore, 1949–1951; R of S 181/47, correspondences between the ROS and STOA, 1946–1978

APPENDIX 3

Membership and presidents of the various trishaw riders' associations from 1947 to 1983

Year	President	Dialect Group	Membership
Singapore Rick and Trishaw Workers Union			
1947	Chng Keng Swee	Hui Ann Hokkien	5,125
1948	Chng Keng Swee	Hui Ann Hokkien	838
1949	Chng Keng Swee	Hui Ann Hokkien	852
Singapore Hired Trishaw Riders' Association			
1950	Chng Keng Swee	Hui Ann Hokkien	Not available
1951	Chng Keng Swee	Hui Ann Hokkien	Not available
1952	Chng Keng Swee	Hui Ann Hokkien	Not available
1953	Chng Keng Swee	Hui Ann Hokkien	Not available
1954	Chng Keng Swee	Hui Ann Hokkien	Not available
1955	Chng Keng Swee	Hui Ann Hokkien	Not available
1956	Chng Keng Swee	Hui Ann Hokkien	Not available
1957	Chng Keng Swee	Hui Ann Hokkien	Not available
1958	Chng Keng Swee	Hui Ann Hokkien	Not available
1959	Chng Keng Swee	Hui Ann Hokkien	Not available
1960	Chng Keng Swee	Hui Ann Hokkien	Not available
1961	Chua Ah Tong	Henghua	360
1962	Chua Ah Tong	Henghua	360
1963	Chua Ah Tong	Henghua	294
1964	Chua Ah Tong	Henghua	310
1965	Chua Ah Tong	Henghua	258
1966	Chua Ah Tong	Henghua	262
1967	Chua Ah Tong	Henghua	246
1968	Chua Ah Tong	Henghua	220
1969	Tong Ah Choon	Henghua	215
1970	Tong Ah Choon	Henghua	206
1971	Tong Ah Choon	Henghua	197
1972	Tong Ah Choon	Henghua	191
1973	Lim Kim Peow	Henghua	178
1974	Lim Kim Peow	Henghua	159

APPENDIX 3

Year	President	Dialect Group	Membership
1975	Lim Kim Peow	Henghua	152
1976	Lim Kim Peow	Henghua	140
1977	Lim Kim Peow	Henghua	153
1978	Lim Kim Peow	Henghua	149
1979	Lim Kim Peow	Henghua	147
1980	Lim Kim Peow	Henghua	124
1981	Lim Kim Peow	Henghua	106
1982	Lim Kim Peow	Henghua	Not available
1983	Lim Kim Peow	Henghua	96

Sources: RMBO 1.328 and RMBO 1.328.2, Annual Returns of the SHTRMBO, 1961–1981; ARSS 1947–1949; NAS, Transcript of A000117/09:83; *The Straits Times*, 01.04.1983

APPENDIX 4

Membership of the Singapore Hired Trishaw Riders' Association by dialect group (1950–1976)

Race	Dialect Group	Sub-Dialect Group	Number
Chinese	Hokchia	---	429
	Henghua	---	347
	Hokkien (Minnanren)	Hui Ann	110
		Cheow Ann	3
		Lam Ann	2
		Tong Ann	2
		Quemoy	2
		Amoy	1
		Ann Kway	1
		Unknown	31
	Teochew	---	29
	Cantonese	---	29
	Foochow	---	4
	Hainanese	---	2
Indian			6
Malay			3
Total Membership between 1950 and 1976			**1,001**

Source: Tabulated from the Membership Registration Book of the SHTRA, 1950–76

APPENDIX 5

Main residential areas of members of the Singapore Hired Trishaw Riders Association (1950–1976)

Street	Post Code	Hokchia	Henghua	Hui Ann	Other Hokkien	Teochew	Cantonese	Total
Desker Road	8	49						49
Duxton Road	2			40			1	41
Muar Road	7	13	21					34
Maude Road	8	33		1				34
Chin Swee Road	3	31		1				32
Anguilla Road	7	21	9					30
Park Road	1	24		1	1		3	29
Prinsep Street	7		29					29
Bencoolen Street	7	6	20	1				27
Sungei Road	8		26					26
Johore Road	7	24					1	25
Jalan Besar	8	17	8					25
Dickson Road	8		22	1		1		24
Upper Weld Road	8	1	22	1				24
Pitt Street	8	23						23
Kelantan Lane	7	21	1					22
Manasseh Lane	3	20				1		21
Middle Road	7		20		1			21
Sam Leong Road	8	20						20
Total		283	198	45	3	2	5	536

Note: These districts were based on the postal code system in use for the past 45 years in Singapore. It was increased from one or two digits to four digits in 1978. With effect from September 1995, it is replaced by a new 6-digit postal code system that has nothing to do with the old system.

Source: Tabulated from the Membership Register Book of the SHTRA, 1950–1976

APPENDIX 6

Residential patterns of the members of the Singapore Hired Trishaw Riders Association (1950–1976)

District Number	Number of Members	Hokchia	Henghua	Hui Ann	Other Hokkiens	Teochew	Cantonese	Others
1	67	27	2	12	3	13	9	1
2	94	8	7	69	3	1	5	1
3	71	60	1	4	2	1	2	1
5	1	-	-	-	-	-	1	-
6	6	1	1	-	1	2	-	1
7	292	111	168	1	4	1	6	1
8	347	194	130	13	5	3	2	-
9	7	2	3	1	-	-	-	1
10	1	-	-	-	1	-	-	-
11	4	-	1	-	1	-	2	-
12	16	6	3	-	2	3	2	-
13	3	-	2	-	-	1	-	-
14	46	6	20	5	13	-	1	1
15	18	9	4	2	2	1	-	-
19	9	2	2	2	2	1	-	-
Address Unavailable	3	1	1	-	-	1	-	-
Address Unclear	16	2	2	1	3	-	-	8
Total	1,001	429	347	110	42	29	29	15

Note: These districts were based on the postal code system in use for the past 45 years in Singapore. It was increased from one or two digits to four digits in 1978. With effect from September 1995, it is replaced by a new 6-digit postal code system that has nothing to do with the old system.

Source: Tabulated from the Membership Register Book of the SHTRA, 1950–1976

APPENDIX 7

Main residential areas of members of the Singapore Hired Trishaw Riders Association (1971–1976)

Street/Area	Post Code	Number of Members	Henghua	Hokchia	Hokkien	Others
Bencoolen Street	7	17	10	6		1
Desker Road	8	13		13		
Geylang (Area)	14	10	4	5	1	
Upper Weld Road	8	8	8			
Havelock Road	3	7	1	6		
Jalan Tenteram	12	7	3	2		2
Weld Road	8	7	7			
Kelantan Lane	8	6	6			
Muar Road	7	6	6			
Prinsep Street	7	6	6			
Toa Payoh (Area)	12	6	2	2	1	1
Ganges Avenue	3	5	3	2		
Pasar Lane	8	5	5			
Race Course Road	8	5		4	1	

Source: Tabulated from two volumes of the SHTRA Monthly Subscription Records Book

APPENDIX 8

Residential patterns of members of the Singapore Hired Trishaw Riders Association (1971–1976)

District Number	Number of Members	Henghua	Hokchia	Hokkien	Teochew	Other Dialect Groups
1	6	2	2		2	
2	2		1	1		
3	21	1	15	2	1	2
7	56	32	20	2		2
8	89	43	43	1	1	1
9	2	1	1			
11	2	1	1			
12	24	12	8	1		3
13	1			1		
14	15	6	7	1	1	
15	7	2	3		1	1
19	2	1	1			
No Address Given	1		1			
Total	228	101	103	9	6	9

Source: Tabulated from two volumes of the SHTRA Monthly Subscription Records Book

APPENDIX 9

Retail price of selected foodstuffs

Foodstuff	Unit*	Annual average in 1947	Annual average in 1951	Average price in November 1960	Average price in October 1972	Average price in March 1983
Beef	1 kati	$1.64	$2.16	$2.00	$2.84	$7.54
Lean pork	1 kati	$2.85	$2.88	$2.25	$2.15	$4.78
Chicken	1 kati	$1.94	$2.14	$1.57	$1.48	$2.35
Eggs	10	$1.67	$1.57	$1.19	$1.11	$1.34
Fish (kurau)	1 kati	$1.82	$2.67	$2.65	$3.48	$12.60
Long beans	1 kati	$0.24	$0.51	$0.38	$0.33	$1.12
Spinach	1 kati	$0.14	$0.24	$0.20	$0.23	$1.04
Bananas (pisang hijau)	10	$0.68	$0.61	$0.60	NA	NA
Large onions	1 kati	$0.30	$0.26	$0.35	$0.34	$0.60
Lard	1 kati	$1.10	$1.25	$0.70	NA	NA
Rice	6 katis	$1.50	$1.65	$1.33	$2.04	$3.61
Sugar	1 kati	$0.26	$0.34	$0.20	$0.40	$0.76
Coffee (ground, tinned)	1 pound	$1.60	$3.27	$1.39	$1.66	$6.34
Tea (Ceylon)	1 pound	$2.85	$2.95	$3.30	$3.04	NA

* Unit – Measure of weights for 1983 were in kilogrammes (1 kati = 1 and 1/3 pounds = 604.8 g). They have been converted into katis and pounds for this table.

Sources: Malayan Statistics: Digest, December 1961; Malayan Statistics: Monthly Digest, May 1951; Malayan Statistics: Monthly Digest, December 1953; Singapore Annual Report 1947

APPENDIX 10

Summary of offences by trishaw riders from 1949 to 1959

Offence	Year	Prosecuted	Convicted	Acquitted
Obstruction	1949	686	617	69
	1950	222	178	44
	1951	100	84	16
	1952	NA	NA	NA
	1953	49	46	3
	1954	168	162	6
	1955	81	79	2
	1956	7	6	1
	1957	5	4	1
	1958	7	5	2
	1959	4	3	1
Loitering	1949	52	46	6
	1950	72	66	6
	1951	23	22	1
	1952	NA	NA	NA
	1953	18	17	1
	1954	33	31	2
	1955	81	79	2
	1956	15	13	2
	1957	4	4	0
	1958	3	1	2
	1959	6	4	2
Failure to wear proper apparel	1949	91	86	5
	1950	442	430	12
	1951	NA	NA	NA
	1952	NA	NA	NA
	1953	NA	NA	NA
	1954	293	267	26
	1955	49	46	3
	1956	7	7	0
	1957	15	13	2
	1958	11	9	2
	1959	7	6	1

APPENDIX 10

Offence	Year	Prosecuted	Convicted	Acquitted
Failure to wear armbadges	1949	274	265	9
	1950	277	269	8
	1951	150	144	6
	1952	NA	NA	NA
	1953	NA	NA	NA
	1954	360	346	14
	1955	45	43	2
	1956	14	13	1
	1957	6	5	1
	1958	62	58	4
	1959	31	27	4
Smoking whilst conveying passengers in trishaws	1949	NA	NA	NA
	1950	NA	NA	NA
	1951	NA	NA	NA
	1952	NA	NA	NA
	1953	NA	NA	NA
	1954	424	403	21
	1955	37	33	4
	1956	10	8	2
	1957	7	5	2
	1958	30	29	1
	1959	23	19	4
Using trishaw to carry goods	1949	NA	NA	NA
	1950	115	110	5
	1951	116	106	10
	1952	NA	NA	NA
	1953	NA	NA	NA
	1954	NA	NA	NA
	1955	284	280	4
	1956	29	29	0
	1957	6	5	1
	1958	4	3	1
	1959	2	2	0
Not having table of fares displayed	1949	10	10	0
	1950	62	57	5
	1951	45	45	0
	1952	NA	NA	NA
	1953	NA	NA	NA
	1954	NA	NA	NA

Offence	Year	Prosecuted	Convicted	Acquitted
	1955	NA	NA	NA
	1956	NA	NA	NA
	1957	NA	NA	NA
	1958	NA	NA	NA
	1959	NA	NA	NA
Behaving in a disorderly manner	1949	12	11	1
	1950	15	12	3
	1951	12	12	0
	1952	NA	NA	NA
	1953	NA	NA	NA
	1954	NA	NA	NA
	1955	NA	NA	NA
	1956	NA	NA	NA
	1957	NA	NA	NA
	1958	NA	NA	NA
	1959	NA	NA	NA
Placing trishaw on foot pavement	1949	NA	NA	NA
	1950	105	105	0
	1951	29	27	2
	1952	NA	NA	NA
	1953	NA	NA	NA
	1954	NA	NA	NA
	1955	NA	NA	NA
	1956	NA	NA	NA
	1957	NA	NA	NA
	1958	NA	NA	NA
	1959	NA	NA	NA
Unlicensed trishaw riders	1949	259	247	12
	1950	305	288	17
	1951	336	322	14
	1952	NA	NA	NA
	1953	262	258	4
	1954	159	157	2
	1955	206	196	10
	1956	32	31	1
	1957	37	37	0
	1958	3	3	0
	1959	1	1	0

Note: Figures for 1952 are not available in all categories.

Sources: ARMCS 1949–1950; ARCCS 1951–1953; ARVRD, 1954–1959

APPENDIX 11

Number of trishaws and trishaw riders

Year	Number of Trishaws	Number of Trishaw Riders
1946*	6,908 + 66	Not available
1947*	8,948 + 43	Approximately 10,000
1948*	8,583 + 30	Not available
1949*	7,892 + 35	8,820
1950*	6,823 + 36	10,951
1951*	5,867 + 32	10,121
1952*	5,093 + 26	5,717
1953*	4,538 + 21	4,958
1954*	4,045 + 19	4,547
1955*	3,809 + 19	4,301
1956*	3,747 + 18	4,328
1957*	3,629 + 16	4,352
1958*	3,627 + 16	4,876
1959*	3,627 + 16	4,816
1960*	3,627 + 4	4,340
1961*	3,629 + 2	3,913
1962*	3,629 + 2	3,612
1963*	3,629 + 2	3,423
1964*	3,629 + 2	3,082
1965*	3,628 + 2	2,730
1966*	3,516 + 2	2,621
1967*	3,516 + 2	2,635
1968*	3,431 + 2	2,844
1969*	3,396 + 1	2,633
1970*	3,388 + 1	2,421
1971*	3,301 + 1	2,247
1972*	2,256 + 1	2,054
1973	3,032	1,880
1974	2,913	1,884
1975	2,773	1,791
1976	2,706	1,861
1977	2,270	1,985

A SLOW RIDE INTO THE PAST

Year	Number of Trishaws	Number of Trishaw Riders
1978	2,197	1,981
1979	1,898	2,032
1980	1,725	2,026
1981	1,607	1,299
1982	Not available	1,348
1983	Not available	968

* Public (Registered and Licenced) Vehicles and Private Vehicles were compiled separately for the years 1946 to 1972.

Sources: ARVRD and ARROV, 1954–1983; Letter addressed to the author from the ROV. Reference ROV/82/379/2-3 dated 29 April 1995.

APPENDIX 12

Accidents involving trishaw riders

Year	Accidents			Number of Accidents of which Cause was Attributed to Public Service Vehicles
	Slight Injury	Serious Injury	Fatal Injury	
1959	177	13	4	63
1960	70	16	3	35
1961	65	18	4	87
1962	77	21	0	44
1963	89	12	5	50
1964	109	16	3	66
1965	83	13	1	37
1966	34	7	1	37
1967	88	9	3	39
1968	57	11	2	16
1969	34	24	3	12
1970	75	16	1	11
1971	38	22	8	16
1972	55	22	5	38

Source: ARVRD, 1959–1972.

APPENDIX 13

Competition between public buses, taxis and trishaws

Year	Number of Public Buses*	Number of Taxis	Number of (Public) Trishaws
1949	448	1,081	7,892
1950	487	1,477	6,823
1951	538	1,534	5,867
1952	622	1,532	5,093
1953	712	1,510	4,538
1954	787	1,512	4,045
1955	839	1,545	3,809
1956	890	1,559	3,747
1957	900	2,328	3,629
1958	907	2,802	3,627
1959	934	3,044	3,627
1960	937	3,145	3,627
1961	1,008	3,188	3,629
1962	1,008	3,142	3,629
1963	1,060	3,185	3,629
1964	1,076	3,204	3,629
1965	1,136	3,206	3,628
1966	1,136	3,483	3,516
1967	1,149	3,752	3,516
1968	1,222	3,808	3,431
1969	1,398	3,794	3,396
1970	1,586	3,784	3,388
1971	1,927	4,809	3,301
1972	2,079	4,884	3,256
1973	2,081	4,942	3,032
1974	2,164	5,162	2,913
1975	2,328	5,338	2,773
1976	2,628	5,473	2,706
1977	2,736	6,009	2,270
1978	2,821	7,683	2,197

APPENDIX 13

Year	Number of Public Buses*	Number of Taxis	Number of (Public) Trishaws
1979	2,894	8,518	1,898
1980	3,003	9,462	1,725
1981	3,003	9,862	1,607
1982	2,682	10,278	N/A
1983	2,766	10,668	N/A

* The 'Number of Public buses' does not include the 50 trolley-buses operational until 1962.

Until 1970, Singapore's public bus service consisted of the government-owned Singapore Traction Company (STC) and 10 other privately-run Chinese bus companies:

1. Green Bus Co. Ltd.
2. Koh Yat Bus Co.
3. Hock Lee Amalgamated Bus Co. Ltd.
4. (Soon Lee and Ngo Hock Bus Companies merged in 1951)
5. Changi Bus Co.
6. Keppel Bus Co. Ltd.
7. Katong Bedok Bus Service Co. Ltd.
8. Ponggol Bus Service
9. Kampong Bahru Bus Service
10. Easy Bus Co.
11. Paya Lebar Bus Co.

In 1971, the STC collapsed due to bankruptcy and all the 10 Chinese companies merged to form three new bus companies:

1. Amalgamated Bus Co. Ltd.
2. Associated Bus Services Pte. Ltd.
3. United Bus Co. Pte. Ltd.

These three companies merged again in 1973 to form the Singapore Bus Service (SBS).

Sources: ARMCS 1949–1950; ARCCS 1951–1953; ARVRD and ARROV, 1954–1983.

APPENDIX 14

The bicycle market of Singapore from 1947 to 1960

Year	Imports	$ '000	Exports	$ '000
1947	36,000 (Approx)	2,540	6,000 (Approx)	490
1948	79,000 (Approx)	5,710	18,000 (Approx)	1,410
1949	81,000 (Approx)	5,520	29,000 (Approx)	2,090
1950	102,000 (Approx)	6,870	36,000 (Approx)	2,580
1951	184,069	13,214	71,921	6,133
1952	288,014	19,858	170,715	13,280
1953	148,919	10,001	54,341	3,963
1954	73,544	6,392	20,439	2,139
1955	72,899	5,896	17,720	1,540
1956	82,567	7,110	16,512	1,545
1957	66,646	5,942	13,885	1,324
1958	51,675	3,909	10,548	1,032
1959	91,300 (Approx)	6,287	13,700 (Approx)	1,151
1960	97,700 (Approx)	7,660	21,300 (Approx)	1,901

Sources: Malayan Statistics: Digest, 1957–1960; Malayan Statistics: Monthly Digest, 1952–1954; Yan 1957

BIBLIOGRAPHY

English language sources

Annual government records (published)

Administration Report of the Municipal Council of Singapore, 1949–1951.
Annual Report of the Registry of Vehicles, 1974.
Annual Report of the Vehicle Registration Department, 1951–1970.
Colony of Singapore Annual Report, 1951.
Colony of Singapore Government Gazette Supplement, 1946–1954.
Malayan Statistics: Digest of Economic and Social Statistics (State of Singapore and Federation of Malaya), 1961.
Malayan Statistics: Monthly Digest, 1951 & 1953.
Singapore Annual Report, 1947.
Singapore Municipal Administration Reports, 1914.
Singapore Year Book, 1968.
Straits Settlements Annual Report, 1949–1951.

Archival materials

British Military Administration. NAS, microfilm BMA 12/46, *Trishaws*, 1946–1950.
City Council. NAS, microfilms NA 461-468, *Minutes of the Proceedings of the City Council of Singapore*, 1952–1956.
Municipal Commission. NAS, microfilms NA 441-445, *Minutes of the Proceedings of the Municipal Commission of Singapore*, 1946–1950.
Labour Department. NAS, microfilm ML 1918, LM 238/46, *Trishaws*, 1946–1947.
Labour Department. NAS, microfilm ML 1919, LM 267/46, *Repatriation of Rickshaw Pullers*, 1946–1947.
Labour Department. NAS, microfilm ML 1927, LM 272/47, *Wearing of Arm Badges by Trishaw Men (Protest Against)*, 1947–1957.
Ministry of Communications. NAS microfilm CI 307, RV 443/5-11 and RV 443/5-11 Vol 2, *Cyclists, Trishas, Jaywalking*, 1973–1977.
Registry of Societies. NAS, microfilm MHA 445, R of S 181/47, *Singapore Trishaw Owners Association*, 1947–1978.
Registry of Trade Unions. NAS, microfilm ML 897, RTU 55, *Singapore Rick and Trishaw Workers Union*, 1946–1950.
Registry of Trade Unions. NAS, microfilm ML 922, RTU 190, *Trishaw Industry*

Proprietors and Manufacturers Association of Singapore, 1950.

Registry of Mutual Benefit Organisations. NAS, microfilm MSA 2962, RMBO 1.328 and RMBO 1.328.2, *Singapore Hired Trishaw Riders Mutual Benefit Organisation*, 1961–1981.

Field interviews

Interview with Mr Chan Kwee Sung at his residence, 20 July 1995.

Newspapers and magazines

China Weekly Review.
Malay Mail.
The Malaya Tribune.
The New Nation.
Singapore Free Press.
The Singapore Tiger Standard.
The Straits Times.
The Syonan Times.

Other primary sources

George Lamb Peet Collection, Murdoch University Library, Perth

Oral history recordings from the Oral History Centre

Chan, Kin Fai. 2005. Accession number A002935/CF1-2.
Fernando, Rennie and Rita. 1998. Accession number A002044/08.
Jumabhoy, Rajabali. 1981. Accession number A000074/37.
Lim, Kim Guan. 1983. Accession number A000280/20.
Namazie, Haji Mohammed Javad. 1983. Accession number A000189/11.
Tan, Richard Swee Guan. 1999. Accession number A002108/08.
Tay, Meng Hock. 1984. Accession number A000470/10.

Books and articles

ARI News 2004, 'Interview with Professor James Warren', 4.

Abeyasekere, Susan (ed) 1985, *From Batavia to Jakarta: Indonesia's Capital 1930s to 1980s*, Monash University, Clayton.

Albers, Patricia C and William R James 1988, 'Travel Photography: A Methodological Approach', *Annals of Tourism Approach*, 15(1).

Anderson, Patrick 1955, *Snake Wine: A Singapore Episode*, Chatto and Windus, London.

Awbery, SS and FW Dalley 1948, *Labour and Trade Union Organization in the Federation of Malaya and Singapore*, Government Press, Kuala Lumpur.

Azuma, Yoshifumi 2001, *The Political Economy of Becak Drivers in Jakarta: A Historical Review*, Working Paper No. 111, Centre of Southeast Asian Studies, Monash Asia

BIBLIOGRAPHY

Institute, Clayton.

Azuma, Yoshifumi 2003, *Urban Peasants: Beca Drivers in Jakarta*, Pustaka Sinar Harapan, Jakarta.

Bariman 1983, *The Socio-Economic Situation of the Trishaw Peddlers in East Java*, Southeast Asia Population Research Awards Programme Report No. 73, Institute of Southeast Asian Studies, Singapore.

Barthes, Roland 1984, *Camera Lucida: Reflections on Photography*, Translated by Richard Howard, Flamingo, London.

Beenhakker, Henri L 1989, 'Non-Motorized Transport in Developing Countries', in *Selected Proceedings of the 5th World Conference on Transport Research at Yokohama, 1989: Transport Policy, Management and Technology towards 2001 (Volume 3: Challenges Facing Transport in Urban and Regional Development and Transport in Developing Countries)*, Western Periodicals, Ventura.

Britton, Nancy Pence 1956, *East of the Sun*, William Blackwood and Sons, Edinburgh.

Burke, Peter 2001, 'Overture. The New History: Its Past and its Future' in Burke, Peter (ed), *New Perspectives on Historical Writing*, second edition, Pennsylvania State University Press, Pennsylvania.

Carstens, Sharon A 1975, *Chinese Associations in Singapore Society: An Examination of Function and Meaning*, Institute of Southeast Asian Studies Occasional Paper No. 37, Singapore.

Case, DJ and JCR Latchford 1981, *A Comparison of Public Transport in Cities in South East Asia*, Overseas Unit of the Transport and Road Research Laboratory, Crowthorne.

Caunce, Stephen 1994, *Oral History and the Local Historian*, Longman, London.

Chan, Chin Bock 1961, 'The Trishaw Won't Last Much Longer', *Singapore Trade*.

Chan, Kwee Sung 2005, *One More Story to Tell: Memories of Singapore, 1930s–1980s*, Landmark Books, Singapore.

Chan, Kwok Bun and Claire Chiang 1994, *Stepping Out: The Making of Chinese Entrepreneurs*, Prentice Hall, Singapore.

Chang, Yong Ching 1973, 'Urban Economics – A New Dimension', in Chua Peng Chye (ed), *Planning in Singapore: Selected Aspects & Issues*, Chopmen Enterprises, Singapore.

Cheng, Homer 1950, 'The Network of Singapore Societies', *Journal of the South Seas Society*, 6(2).

Cheng, Lim Keak 1985, *Social Change and the Chinese in Singapore: A Socio-Economic Geography With Special Reference to* Bang *Structure*, Singapore University Press, Singapore.

Cheng, Lim Keak 1990, 'Reflections on the Changing Roles of Chinese Clan Associations in Singapore', *Asian Culture*, 14.

Cheng, Lim Keak 1993, 'The Xinghua Community in Singapore: A Study of the Socio-Economic Adjustment of a Minority Group' in Suryadinata, Leo (ed), *Chinese*

Adaptation and Diversity: Essays On Society and Literature In Indonesia, Malaysia and Singapore, Singapore University Press, Singapore.

Cheng, Lim Keak 1995, 'Chinese Clan Associations in Singapore: Social Change and Continuity' in Suryadinata, Leo (ed), *Southeast Asian Chinese: The Socio-Cultural Dimension*, Times Academic Press, Singapore.

Chia, Felix 1984, *Reminiscences*, Magro International, Singapore.

Chiew, Seen Kong 1995, 'The Chinese in Singapore: From Colonial Times to the Present' in Suryadinata, Leo (ed), *Southeast Asian Chinese: The Socio-Cultural Dimension*, Times Academic Press, Singapore.

Chin, Hoong Chor 1998, 'Urban Transport Planning in Singapore' in Yuen, Belinda (ed), *Planning Singapore: From Plan to Implementation*, Singapore Institute of Planners, Singapore.

Chinese Heritage Editorial Committee 1990, *Chinese Heritage*, Singapore Federation of Chinese Clan Associations and EPB Publishers, Singapore.

Cohen, Eric, Yeshayahu Nir and Uri Almagor 1992, 'Stranger-Local Interaction in Photography', *Annals of Tourism Research*, 19(2).

Colony of Singapore 1949, *Report of the Special Committee to Advise on Parking Problems*, Legislative Council Paper No. 150, Singapore.

Colony of Singapore 1955a, *Master Plan: Reports of Study Groups and Working Parties*, Government Printing Office, Singapore.

Colony of Singapore 1955b, *Master Plan: Report of Survey*, Government Printing Office, Singapore.

Colony of Singapore 1956, *Report of the Commission of Inquiry into the Public Passenger Transport System of Singapore*, Government Printing Office, Singapore.

Crissman, Lawrence W 1967, 'The Segmentary Structure of Urban Overseas Chinese Communities', *Man*, 2(2).

Department of Social Welfare 1947, *A Social Survey of Singapore: A Preliminary Study of Some Aspects of Social Conditions In the Municipal Area of Singapore, December 1947*, Department of Social Welfare, Singapore.

Del Tufo, MV 1949, *Malaya: A Report of the 1947 Census of Population*, Crown Agents for the Colonies on behalf of the Governments of the Federation of Malaya and the Colony of Singapore, London.

Dick, HW 1981a, 'Urban Public Transport: Jakarta, Surabaya and Malang – Part I', *Bulletin of Indonesian Economic Studies*, 17(1).

Dick, HW 1981b, 'Urban Public Transport: Jakarta, Surabaya and Malang – Part II', *Bulletin of Indonesian Economic Studies*, 17(2).

Dick, HW and PJ Rimmer 1986, 'Urban Public Transport In Southeast Asia: A Case Study In Technological Imperialism?', *Rivista Internationale dei Transporti* [International Journal of Transport Economics], 13(2).

Dick, HW and PJ Rimmer 2003, *Cities, Transport and Communications: The Integration of*

BIBLIOGRAPHY

Southeast Asia since 1850, Palgrave Macmillan, Basingstoke.

Dick, Howard 2005, 'Crisis and Continuity: The Resilience of the Small-scale Transport Sector on Java, 1890–1990s', in Thee Kian Wie (ed), *The Asia-Pacific Century in Historical Perspective*, Indonesian Institute of Sciences, Jakarta.

Dobbs, Stephen 2003, *The Singapore River: A Social History, 1819–2002*, Singapore University Press, Singapore.

Ee, Joyce 1961, 'Chinese Migration to Singapore', *Journal of Southeast Asian History*, 2(1).

Fong Sip Chee 1979, *The PAP Story: The Pioneering Years*, Times Periodicals, Singapore.

Forbes, Dean 1978, 'Urban-Rural Interdependence: The Trishaw Riders of Ujung Pandang' in Rimmer, PJ, DW Drakakis-Smith and TG McGee (eds), *Food, Shelter and Transportation in Southeast Asia and the Pacific*, Australian National University, Canberra.

Gamba, Charles 1954, 'Some Social Problems in Singapore', *The Australian Quarterly*, 26(2).

Gamba, Charles 1962, *The Origins of Trade Unionism In Malaya: A Study In Colonial Labour Unrest*, Eastern Universities Press, Singapore.

Gamer, Robert E 1972, *The Politics of Urban Development in Singapore*, Oxford University Press, Singapore.

Gilderhaus, Mark T 1992, *History and Historians: A Historiographical Introduction*, second edition, Prentice Hall, Englewood Cliffs.

Gilmour, OW 1950, *With Freedom to Singapore*, Ernest Benn, London.

Gopalakrishnan, V and Anada Perera 1983, *Singapore – Changing Landscapes: Geylang, Chinatown, Serangoon*, FEP International and Singapore Broadcasting Corporation, Singapore.

Gould, Harold A 1965, 'Lucknow Rickshawallas: The Social Organization of An Occupational Category', *International Journal of Comparative Sociology*, 6(1).

Grice, Kevin and David Drakakis-Smith 1985, 'The Role of the State In Shaping Development: Two Decades of Growth In Singapore', *Transactions of the Institute of British Geographers*, 10.

Ho, Kong Chong and Valerie Lim Nyuk Eun 1992, 'Backlanes as Contested Regions: Construction and Control of Physical Space' in Chua Beng Huat and Norman Edwards (eds), *Public Space: Design, Use and Management*, Singapore University Press, Singapore.

Ho, Ruth 1975, *Rainbow Round My Shoulder*, Eastern Universities Press, Singapore.

Housing and Development Board 1970, *First Decade in Public Housing 1960–69*, Housing and Development Board, Singapore.

Hsieh, Jiann 1978, 'The Chinese Community in Singapore: The Internal Structure and Its Basic Constituents' in Peter SJ Chen and Hans-Dieter Evans (eds), *Studies in ASEAN Sociology: Urban Society and Social Change*, Chopmen Publishers, Singapore.

Inside Indonesia 1990, 'Leave Our Becaks Alone', 22.

Josey, Alex 1954, *Trade Unionism in Malaya*, Donald Moore, Singapore.

Jumabhoy, R 1970, *Multiracial Singapore*, Tak Seng Press, Singapore.

Kartodirdjo, Sartono 1981, *The Pedicab in Yogyakarta: A Study of Low Cost Transportation and Poverty Problems*, Gadjah Mada University Press, Yogyakarta.

Kaye, Barrington 1960, *Upper Nankin Street Singapore: A Sociological Study of Chinese Households Living In a Densely Populated Area*, University of Malaya Press, Singapore.

Khoo, Gilbert 1981, 'The Becamen of Kelantan', *Malaysian Panorama*, 11(4).

Kirkup, James 1969, *Streets of Asia*, J M Dent and Sons, London.

Laquian, Aprodicio A 2005, *Beyond Metropolis: The Planning and Governance of Asia's Mega-Urban Regions*, Woodrow Wilson Center Press, Washington DC and The John Hopkins University Press, Baltimore.

Lee, Edwin 1986, 'The Historiography of Singapore' in Kapur, Basant K (ed), *Singapore Studies: Critical Surveys of the Humanities and Social Sciences*, Singapore University Press, Singapore.

Lee, Edwin 1989, 'The Colonial Legacy' in Sandhu, Kernial Singh and Paul Wheatley (eds), *Management of Success: The Moulding of Modern Singapore*, Institute of Southeast Asian Studies, Singapore.

Lian, Kwen Fee 1992, 'Review Essay: In Search of a History of Singapore?', *Southeast Asian Journal of Social Science*, 20(1).

Lim, Jason 1996, 'The Trishaw Industry as a "*Bang*"-Based Trade', *Journal of the Malaysian Branch of the Royal Asiatic Society*, 69(2).

Lim, Jason 2005, 'Memories of a Community-Based Occupation: What Trishaw Riders Remember about Their Trade, 1942–1968' in National Archives of Singapore (ed), *Reflections and Interpretations: Oral History Centre 25th Anniversary Publication*, Oral History Centre, Singapore.

Lim, William SW 1980, *An Alternative Urban Strategy*, DP Architects, Singapore.

Lim, William Siew Wai 1975, *Equity and Urban Environment in the Third World: With Special Reference to ASEAN Countries and Singapore*, DP Consultant Service, Singapore.

Logan, William S 2002, 'Introduction: Globalization, Cultural Identity, and Heritage' in Logan, William S (ed), *The Disappearing 'Asian' City: Protecting Asia's Urban Heritage in a Globalizing World*, Oxford University Press, Oxford.

Low, NI 1973, *When Singapore Was Syonan-To*, Eastern Universities Press, Singapore.

Mak, Lau Fong 1995, *The Dynamics of Chinese Dialect Groups in Early Malaya*, Singapore Society of Asian Studies, Singapore.

McGee, TG 1967, *The Southeast Asian City: A Social Geography of the Primate Cities of Southeast Asia*, G Bell and Sons, London.

McKie, Ronald 1963, *Malaysia in Focus*, Angus and Robertson, Sydney.

McKie, Ronald 1972, *Singapore*, Angus and Robertson, Sydney.

Meier, Alan K 1977, 'Becaks, Bemos, Lambros and Productive Pandemonium', *Technology Review*, 79(3).

BIBLIOGRAPHY

Moore, Donald 1954, *Far Eastern Agent: Or the Diary of an Eastern Nobody*, Hodder and Stoughton, London.

Moore, Donald 1955, *We Live in Singapore*, Hodder and Stoughton, London.

Moore, Donald (ed) 1956, *Where Monsoons Meet: The Story of Malaya in the Form of An Anthology*, George G Harrap and Co, London.

MRT Review Team 1980, *Singapore Transport and Urban Development Options*, MRT Review Team, Singapore.

Murray, Alison J 1991, *No Money, No Honey: A Study of Street Traders and Prostitutes in Jakarta*, Oxford University Press, Singapore.

Mydin, Iskander 1992, 'Historical Images – Changing Audiences' in Edwards, Elizabeth (ed), *Anthropology and Photography, 1860–1920*, Yale University Press, New Haven, in association with the Royal Anthropological Institute, London.

Newman, Peter and Andy Thornley 2005, *Planning World Cities: Globalization and Urban Politics*, Palgrave Macmillan, Basingstoke.

Ommanney, FD 1960, *Eastern Windows*, Longmans, Green and Co, London.

Oral History Department 1990, *Recollections: People and Places*, Oral History Department, Singapore.

Owen, Wilfred 1972, *The Accessible City*, The Brookings Institution, Washington DC.

Pendakur, V Setty 1984, *Urban Transport in ASEAN*, Institute of Southeast Asian Studies, Singapore.

Provisional Mass Rapid Transit Authority 1981, *Republic of Singapore Comprehensive Traffic Study Phase A: Summary Report*, Wilbur Smith and Associates, Singapore.

Purcell, Victor 1965, *The Memoirs of a Malayan Official*, Cassell and Co, London.

Raffles Institution Interact Club 1978, 'The Trishaw Rider', n.p.

Rajaratnam, S 1987, 'Singapore: Global City (1972)', in Chan Heng Chee and Obaid ul Haq (eds), *S Rajaratnam – The Prophetic & the Political: Selected Speeches & Writings of S Rajaratnam*, Graham Brash, Singapore.

Replogle, Michael A 1989, 'Transportation Strategies for Sustainable Development', in *Selected Proceedings of the 5th World Conference on Transport Research at Yokohama, 1989: Transport Policy, Management and Technology Towards 2001 (Volume 3: Challenges Facing Transport in Urban and Regional Development and Transport in Developing Countries)*, Western Periodicals, Ventura.

Rimmer, Peter J 1978, 'The Future of Trishaw Enterprises in Penang', in Rimmer, PJ, DW Drakakis-Smith and TG McGee (eds), *Food, Shelter and Transportation in Southeast Asia and the Pacific*, Australian National University, Canberra.

Rimmer, Peter J 1982a, 'Theories and Techniques in Third World Settings: Trishaw Pedallers and *Towkays* in Georgetown, Malaysia', *Australian Geographer*, 15(3).

Rimmer, Peter J 1982b, 'Urban Public Transport in Smaller Malaysian Towns: Threat to the Trishaw Industry', *Malaysian Journal of Tropical Geography*, 5.

Rimmer, Peter J 1986, *Rikisha to Rapid Transit: Urban Public Transport Systems and Policy in Southeast Asia*, Pergamon Press, Sydney.

Rimmer, Peter J 1988, 'The Triad In East and Southeast Asian Transport: Corporatisation, Privatisation and Deregulation', in *13th Australasian Transport Research Forum: Forum Papers Volume 2*, Ministry of Transport, Christchurch.

Rimmer, Peter J and Howard Dick 2009, *The City in Southeast Asia: Patterns, Processes and Policy*, NUS Press, Singapore.

Rimmer, Peter J, Lenore Manderson and Colin Barlow 1990, 'The Underside of Malaysian History' in Rimmer, Peter J and Lisa M Allen (eds), *The Underside of Malaysian History: Pullers, Prostitutes, Plantation Workers*, Singapore University Press, Singapore.

Safran, William 1991, 'Diasporas in Modern Societies: Myths of Homeland and Return', *Diaspora*, 1(1).

Savage, Victor R 1992a, 'Landscape Change: From Kampung to Global City' in Singh, Avijit and John Pitts (eds), *Physical Adjustments in a Changing Landscape: The Singapore Story*, Singapore University Press, Singapore.

Savage, Victor R 1992b, 'Street Culture in Colonial Singapore' in Chua Beng Huat and Norman Edwards (eds), *Public Space: Design, Use and Management*, Singapore University Press, Singapore.

Scherer, Joanna C 1992, 'The Photographic Document: Photographs as Primary Data In Anthropological Enquiry' in Edwards, Elizabeth (ed), *Anthropology and Photography, 1860–1920*, Yale University Press, New Haven, in association with the Royal Anthropological Institute, London.

Scott, James C 1998, *Seeing Like a State: How Certain Schemes to Improve the Human Condition Have Failed*, Yale University Press, New Haven.

Seah, Chee Meow 1985, 'Public Transportation' in Quah, Jon ST, Chan Heng Chee and Seah Chee Meow (eds), *Government and Politics of Singapore*, Oxford University Press, Singapore.

Singapore Housing Committee 1947, *Report of the Singapore Housing Committee*, Government Printing Office, Singapore.

Sit, Yin Fong 1983, *Tales of Chinatown*, Heinemann Asia, Singapore.

Smithies, Michael 1982, *A Javanese Boyhood: An Ethnographic Biography*, Federal Publications, Singapore.

Socio-Economic Research and Central Planning Unit 1979, *A Socio-Economic Study of Trishawmen in Pulau Pinang*, Socio-Economic Research and Central Planning Unit, Kuala Lumpur.

Soegijoko, Budhy Tjahjati S 1984, 'Becaks as a Component of Urban Public Transportation in Indonesia', *Prisma*, 32.

Spencer, AH 1988, 'Modernization and Incorporation: The Development of Singapore's Bus Services, 1945–1974', *Environment and Planning A*, 20(8).

BIBLIOGRAPHY

Spencer, Andrew 1989, 'Urban Transport' in Leinbach, Thomas R and Chia Lin Sien (eds), *South-East Asian Transport: Issues in Development*, Oxford University Press, Singapore.

Stenson, Michael R 1970, *Industrial Conflict in Malaya: Prelude to the Communist Revolt of 1948*, Oxford University Press, London.

Suyama, Taku 1962, 'Pang Societies and the Economy of Chinese Immigrants In Southeast Asia' in Tregonning, KG (ed), *Papers on Malayan History*, University of Malaya in Singapore, Singapore.

Swinstead, Gene and George Haddon 1981, *Singapore Stopover*, Times Books International, Singapore.

Tan, Lee Wah 1975, 'Changes In the Distribution of the Population of Singapore, 1957–1970', *The Journal of Tropical Geography*, 40.

Tan, Thomas TW 1986, 'Voluntary Associations As A Model of Social Change', *Southeast Asian Journal of Social Science*, 14(2).

Tan, Thomas Tsu-Wee 1990, *Chinese Dialect Groups: Traits and Trades*, Opinion Books, Singapore.

Tanjong Pagar Citizen's Consultative Committee 1989, *Tanjong Pagar: Singapore's Cradle of Development*, Tanjong Pagar Citizen's Consultative Committee, Singapore.

Textor, Robert B 1961, *From Peasant to Pedicab Driver: A Social Study of Northeastern Thai Farmers Who Periodically Migrated to Bangkok and Became Pedicab Drivers*, second edition, Yale University Southeast Asia Studies Cultural Report Series No. 9, New Haven.

Thomas, TH 1981, *Rickshaws In Calcutta*, UNNAYAN, Calcutta.

Thompson, Paul 1988, *The Voice of the Past: Oral History*, second edition, Oxford University Press, Oxford.

Tong, Chee Kiong 1993, 'The Inheritance of the Dead: Mortuary Rituals Among the Chinese In Singapore', *Southeast Asian Journal of Social Science*, 21(2).

Turnbull, CM 2009, *A History of Modern Singapore 1819–2005*, NUS Press, Singapore.

Tyner, James 2003. 'Cities of Southeast Asia', in Brunn, Stanley D, Jack F Williams and Donald J Zeigler, *Cities of the World: World Regional Urban Development*, third edition, Rowman and Littlefield, Lanham.

Van Cuylenburg, John Bertram 1982, *Singapore through Sunshine and Shadow: Recollections of Old Singapore*, Heinemann Asia, Singapore.

Varaprasad, N 1989, 'Providing Mobility and Accessibility' in Sandhu, Kernial Singh and Paul Wheatley (eds), *Management of Success: The Moulding of Modern Singapore*, Institute of Southeast Asian Studies, Singapore.

Walters, DK 1937, *The Municipal Ordinance of the Straits Settlements*, Government Printing Office, Singapore.

Warren, James Francis 1986, *Rickshaw Coolie: A People's History of Singapore (1880–1940)*, Oxford University Press, Singapore.

Warren, James Francis 1995, 'A Strong Stomach and Flawed Material: Towards the Making of a Trilogy, Singapore, 1870–1940', *Southeast Asian Studies*, 33(2).

Warren, Jim 1985, 'Social History and the Photograph: Glimpses of the Singapore Rickshaw Coolie in the Early 20th Century', *Journal of the Malaysian Branch of the Royal Asiatic Society*, 58(1).

Wilson, JLJ (ed) 1956, 'The Asian City', *Current Affairs Bulletin*, 19(5).

Yao, Souchou 1984, 'Why Chinese Voluntary Associations: Structure or Function', *Journal of the South Seas Society*, 39(1 & 2).

Yee, Joseph 1973, 'Urban Transport Modes – The Way Ahead', in Chua Peng Chye (ed), *Planning in Singapore: Selected Aspects & Issues*, Chopmen Enterprises, Singapore.

Yen, Ching-hwang 1986, *A Social History of the Chinese in Singapore and Malaya, 1800–1911*, Oxford University Press, Singapore.

Yeoh, Brenda SA and Lau Wei Peng 1995, 'Historic District, Contemporary Meanings: Urban Conservation and the Creation and Consumption of Landscape Spectacle in Tanjong Pagar' in Yeoh, Brenda SA and Lily Kong (eds), *Portraits of Places: History, Community and Identity in Singapore*, Times Editions, Singapore.

Yong, CF 1992, *Chinese Leadership and Power in Colonial Singapore*, Times Academic Press, Singapore.

Yong, CF 1987, *Tan Kah Kee: The Making of an Overseas Chinese Legend*, Oxford University Press, Singapore.

Zunz, Olivier 1985, 'Introduction' in Zunz, Olivier (ed), *Reliving the Past: The Worlds of Social History*, University of North Carolina Press, Chapel Hill.

Unpublished materials and theses

Chan Kwee Sung 1995a, 'Back to British Rule: Military Administration', unpublished.

Chan Kwee Sung 1995b, 'Trishaw Cyclists', unpublished.

Cooper, Dave Cooper 1991, 'Postcards from Paradise and Other Icons of the Tourist Age', BA (Honours) thesis in Asian Studies, Murdoch University.

Eio Cheng Kiang 1979, 'The Development of the Road Network and the Public Bus Services In Singapore', Academic exercise for BA (Honours) in Geography, University of Singapore.

Forbes, Dean Keith 1979, 'Development and the 'Informal' Sector: A Study of Pedlars and Trishaw Riders In Ujung Pandang, Indonesia', PhD thesis in Geography, Monash University.

Siddiqi, ZM Shahid 1967, 'The Registration and Deregistration of Trade Unions In Singapore', Master of Laws thesis, University of Singapore.

Sim Beng Huat 1975, 'Public Passenger Transportation in Singapore', Academic Exercise for a BA (Honours) in Geography, University of Singapore.

BIBLIOGRAPHY

Teo, Peggy Cheok Chin 1982, 'The Mental Image of Package Tourists: A Study of Singapore's Tourist Attractions', MA thesis in Geography, National University of Singapore.

Wee Soo Hup 1962, 'The Trisha Riders' Population in Singapore', Academic exercise for BA (Hons) in Social Studies, University of Singapore.

Yeo, Lian Bee Katherine 1989, 'Hawkers and the State in Colonial Singapore: Mid-Nineteenth Century to 1939', MA thesis in History, Monash University.

Mandarin language and dialect sources

Archival materials

National Archives of Singapore.

Monthly Subscription Book, Membership Register, Vehicle Register and Minutes of Annual General and Executive Committee Meetings of the Singapore Hired Trishaw Riders Association, 1950–1976, microfilm NA 565.

Oral history recordings from the Oral History Centre

Anonymous 25. 2000. Accession number B002294/09.
Chia Kee Huat 1983. Accession number A000358/09.
Foong Lai Kum (Madam) 1999. Accession number A002226/12.
Goh Leng Huat & Yeo Yan Ngoh (Madam) 2001. Accession number A002493/36.
Koh Boon Chai 1998. Accession number A002009/08.
Koh Teong Koo 1981. Accession number A000136/06.
Lee Oi Wah (Madam) 1999. Accession number A002217/09.
Lim Hong Cher 1986. Accession number A000745/06.
Lim Tiang Lin 1997. Accession number A001870/12.
Low Teck Cheng 1998. Accession number A002034/13.
Lu Tian Lee 1986. Accession number A000669/16.
Ng Kah Eng 1981. Accession number A000117/09.
Tan Ai Mai 1981. Accession number A000132/05.
Tan Low Kee 1988. Accession number A000895/06.
Tay Quay Muay 1986. Accession number A000739/03.
Wee Jong Dit 1998. Accession number A002028/14.

Registry of Societies

Article 4, Chapter 1 of the Constitution of the Singapore Hockposian Association obtained on 11 August 1995.

Field recordings

Interview with 'Ah Tong' outside Singapore Futsing Association, 12 July 1995.

Interview with Madam Ong Chwee Lan, bicycle shop owner, 14 July 1995.

Newspapers
Lianhe Zaobao 联合早报.
Nanyang Siang Pau 南洋商报.
Sin Chew Jit Poh 星洲日报.

Books and articles
Chen Weilong 陈维龙 1967, '*Li Guangqian Zhuan* 李光前传 [A Biography of Lee Kong Chian]', *Journal of the South Seas Society*, 22(1 & 2).

Cheng Guangyu 程光裕 1987, 'Yihexuan Shouren Zongli Li Tuiqian – Yiwei Xinjiapo Huaqiao Lingxiu Zhichi Zhongguo Geming Zhi Shishi Chutan' 怡和轩首任总理林推进～一位新加坡华侨领袖支持中国革命之史事初探 [Lin T'ui-Chien, the first president of Ee H-oe Hean: A preliminary discussion of an overseas Chinese leader at Singapore, who supported the Chinese revolution], *Guoshiguan Guankan* 国史馆馆刊, 3.

Cui Guiqiang 崔贵强 1994, *Xinjiapo Huaren: Chong Kaibu Dao Jianguo* 新加坡华人：从开埠到建国 [The Chinese in Singapore: Past and Present], Singapore Federation of Chinese Clan Associations and EPB Publishers, Singapore.

Li Jingfu 黎经富 1968, '*Xinjiapo De Renkou Zengjia Yu Renkou Gouzao De Bianhua* 新加坡的人口增加与人口构造的变化 [Population Increase and Structural Changes in Singapore]', *Nanyang University Journal*, 2.

Lin Xiaosheng 林孝胜 1987, 'Li Guangqian De Qiye Wangguo (1927–1954): Xinhua Jiazu Qiye Gean Yanjiu' 李光前的企业王国 (1927–1954)：新华家族企业个案研究 [The business empire of Lee Kong Chian: A case study of Singapore Chinese family business], *Asian Culture*, 9.

Lin Xiaosheng 林孝胜 1990, 'Chen Liushi De Jiazu Qiye Pouxi – Xinjiapo Huaren Jiazu Qiye Gean Yanjiu' 陈六使的家族企业剖析～新加坡华人家族企业个案研究 [An analysis of the family enterprise of Tan Lark Sye], *Huaqiao Huaren Lishi Yanjiu* 华侨华人历史研究, 2.

Nanyang Daxue 南洋大学 (Nanyang University) 1956, *Nanyang Daxue Chuangxiaoshi* 南洋大学创校史 [Founding of Nanyang University], Nanyang Wenhua Chubanshe, Singapore.

Ou Rubo 区如伯 1991, *Zuxian De Hangye* 祖先的行业 [The Trades of Our Ancestors], Seng Yew Book Store, Singapore.

Ou Rubo 区如伯 1992, *Bainian Shuren* 百年树人 [The Nurturing of a Generation], Seng Yew Book Store, Singapore.

Peng Song Toh 1983, *Directory of Associations in Singapore, 1982–83*. Historical Culture Publishers, Singapore.

Qiu Xinmin 邱新民 1990, *Xinjiapo Fengwu Waiji* 新加坡风物外记 [An Account of

BIBLIOGRAPHY

Singapore's Past], Seng Yew Book Store, Singapore.
Singapore Futsing Association 新加坡福清会馆 1982, *Xinjiapo Fuqing Huiguan Qishi Zhounian Jinian Kan 1910–1980* 新加坡福清会馆七十周年纪念刊 [70th Anniversary Souvenir Magazine of the Singapore Futsing Association], Singapore Futsing Association, Singapore.
Wu Hua 吴华 1975, *Xinjiapo Huazu Huiguan Zhi (1)* 新加坡华族会馆志(1) [History of the Chinese Clan Associations (1)], South Seas Society, Singapore.
Yan Qinghuang 颜清湟 1991. '*Chong Lishi Jiaodu Kan Xinma Zongqinghui De Fazhan He Qiantu* 从历史角度看新马宗亲会的发展和前途 [The Future and Development of Clan Associations in Singapore and Malaysia from a Historical Perspective]', *Asian Culture*, 15.
Yan Qinghuang 颜清湟 2005, *Haiwai Huaren De Shehui Bianqe Yu Shangye Chengzhang* 海外华人的社会变革与商业成长 [Social transformation and commercial growth of the overseas Chinese], Xiamen University Press, Xiamen.
Yan Renshan 严仁山 (ed) 1957, *Singapore Cycle and Motor Traders' Association Silver Jubilee Souvenir*, Singapore Cycle and Motor Traders' Association, Singapore.
Yan Renshan 严仁山 (ed) 1972, *Hin Ann Huay Kuan 50th Anniversary Souvenir Issue 1970*, Hin Ann Huay Kuan, Singapore.
Yan Qinghuang 颜清湟 1991. '*Chong Lishi Jiaodu Kan Xinma Zongqinghui De Fazhan He Qiantu* 从历史角度看新马宗亲会的发展和前途 [The Future and Development of Clan Associations in Singapore and Malaysia from a Historical Perspective]', *Asian Culture*, 15.
Yang Meijing 杨美景 1996, '*Lun Chen Jiageng De Huaqiao Touzi Guan*' 论陈嘉庚的华侨投资观 [An analysis of Tan Kah Kee's view on overseas Chinese investment], *Nanyang Wenti Yanjiu* 南洋问题研究, 3.
Zhong Baoxian 钟宝贤 2002. '*Yige "Huaqiao Jiazu" De Dansheng – Yu Dongxuan Jiazu De Sandai Yanbian*' 一个'华侨家族'的诞生~余东旋家族的三代演变 [The birth of an "overseas Chinese family": Three generations of the Eu Tong Sen family], *Asian Culture*, 26.

Unpublished materials

Nanyang Daxue Lishi Xi 南洋大学历史系 (Nanyang University History Department) 1971, *Xinghuaren Yu Jiaotong Hangye (1880–1971)* 兴化人与交通行业 [The Henghua People and the Transport Industry], unpublished.

INDEX

1955 Singapore Master Plan   102–3, 107, 113

bang   xx, 38–60, 124
Bangkok   1–2, 5, 6, 7, 9, 11
bicycle industry   34, 41–2, 108, 111–2,
bicycle shop owners   33–4, 36–7 *see also* trishaw owners
British Military Administration (BMA)   17–9, 36–7, 44, 58, 106 , 125
bus companies   xix, 58, 109–10
buses   9, 12, 41, 79, 108–10, 114, 121, 124

Cantonese   38, 52
Chinatown   33, 45, 51–3, 79–80, 83, 95, 108, 113–6, 118, 121
Chinese, the   *see* Overseas Chinese
Chinese Affairs Secretariat   18–23, 100
Chung Hwa Free Clinic   82, 107, 120
City Council, the   xix, 101–4
colonial authorities   xviii, 17–20, 31, 37, 51, 59–60, 82, 95–6, 98, 109, 124

employment   2, 10, 29, 30–1, 39–40, 93–4, 104–5, 115–7

Foochows   38, 51, 95
Fujian   38, 40–1, 43, 125
fund-raising activities   48, 82–7, 107, 124–5

Geylang   51, 93, 97, 114
Guangdong   38

Hainanese   38–9
Hakka   38
Henghuas   xvii, xix–xx, 4, 33, 38–41, 44, 50–1, 59, 81, 90, 95, 111, 124–6
Hin Ann Huay Kuan   41
Hock Leong Hin Company   23, 41
Hock Sin Hin Chop   47–8
Hokchias (Hokchengs)   xx, 4, 33, 38–43, 50–1, 59, 81, 84, 90, 124–6
Hokkien Huay Kuan   41, 43, 82

Hokkiens (Minnanren)   38, 40, 42–4, 81, 126
Housing and Development Board (HDB)   96, 108, 112–5
Hui Ann Association   43

inner city   45, 51–3, 79–80, 108, 111, 113–5, 125

Japanese Military Administration   14, 36–7
Japanese Occupation, the   xx, 14–9, 26, 28, 33, 36, 39, 43–4, 56, 88, 97, 109, 118, 124
Joo Chiat Road/Katong area   47–8, 51, 81, 83, 92–3, 114
Jumahboy, Rajabali (a municipal commissioner)   26, 30, 98–9
Jurong   108, 111, 114–5

Kang Tou Ong Clansmen Association 42

Labour Front (LF) government (1956–1959)   35, 103, 106
land transport system *see* public transportation
Laycock, John (a municipal commissioner)   27–9
Lim Kim San   85
Lim Yew Hock government *see* LF government
Little India   51, 81, 108, 115, 118, 121

Master Plan *see* 1955 Singapore Master Plan
migration   xviii, xix, 3–4, 7, 9, 39, 50
modernisation, symbols of   10, 12–3, 29, 101, 111–2, 123 *see also* urbanisation
motorised trishaws   9–10, 101–2, 111
Municipal Commission (also Municipal Council)   xix, 9, 14, 26–30, 34, 53, 55, 96–102, 106, 110, 124
mutual aid   39–42, 57–8, 125 *see also* Singapore Hired Trishaw Riders Mutual Benefit Organisation (SHTRMBO)

Nanyang University xvii, 48, 82, 86, 94–5, 107, 124
National Defence Fund 82, 85–7, 107, 124

opium users 31, 53
Overseas Chinese, characteristics of xv–xvii, xx, 28, 38–40, 52–3, 59, 79, 82, 84–5, 94, 125 *see also bang*

pedicab drivers *see* trishaw riders
pedicabs *see* trishaws
Penang 1–2, 4–6, 8, 11
People's Action Party (PAP) government, the (1959–present) 9, 98, 103–4, 106, 108, 112
petrol shortages 15, 36, 110
public transportation
    planning 9, 12, 102–3, 106–7, 109–15
    problems of 110–1
    public opinion of 9–13, 29–30, 101–3, 110

Registrar of Vehicles (ROV) 25, 56, 98, 104–5, 111, 115, 117
rickshaw industry xix, 14–5, 25–33, 37, 40–1
    abolition of xx, 4, 25–7, 30, 37, 42, 49, 125
rickshaw pullers xvii–xviii, xix, 4, 8, 27, 30–3, 36–7, 40–3, 50, 59, 79, 125
    repatriation of 30–3
Road Transport Department (RTD) 18–23, 29–30, 35–7

Shantou 30–1
Singapore Census 39, 43, 49
Singapore Chinese *see* Overseas Chinese
Singapore Chinese Chamber of Commerce (SCCC) 83–4, 102
Singapore Futsing Association 42
Singapore Hired Trishaw Riders Association (SHTRA) xix–xx, 8, 36, 47, 48, 56–60, 82–6, 94, 101, 104–6, 110, 116, 118–21, 125
Singapore Hired Trishaw Riders Mutual Benefit Organisation (SHTRMBO) 57–8, 119–20, 125
Singapore Rickshaw and Trishaw Workers Union (SRTWU) 31–2, 56–7, 59–60, 99–100
Singapore River, the xviii, 43, 106
Singapore Tricycle Workers Mutual Help Association 18, 20–4

Singapore Trishaw Owners Association (STOA) xix–xx, 20–1, 44–9, 56–7, 83, 86, 101–2, 105–7, 118, 124
Societies Ordinance, the 44, 46
strikes 58–60, 100–1

taxis xix, 12, 28, 41, 58–9, 79, 92, 108–10, 121, 124
Teck Huat Tricycle Company 45
Teochews 38, 40
tourism industry 51–2, 92, 112–3, 115–8, 121–2
Trade Unions Ordinance, the 45–6
travellers' impressions/accounts xix–xx, 3, 87–92, 112–3
trishaw
    accidents involving 10–1, 91–2, 111
    as a means of inner city/local transit xix, 4–5, 8, 10–1, 36–7, 51, 58, 79–81, 101, 106–7, 109, 114–5, 121
    design and manufacture of 1–2, 15, 33–6, 111–2
    road restrictions on 2, 9–11, 101–6, 121, 124
trishaw industry in Singapore
    associations/unions *see* SHTRA, STOA, SHTRMBO, SRTWU and TIPMAS
    development of the xvi, xix–xxi, 1–3, 14–37, 42–3, 59, 79, 87–90, 108–25
    regulation and control of 18–23, 35–7, 48–9, 54, 97–107, 121–3
Trishaw Industry Proprietors and Manufacturers Association of Singapore (TIPMAS) 45–6, 101–2
trishaw owners 19–25, 34, 36, 43–9, 57, 125
trishaw riders
    alleged criminal activities 49, 94–7, 117, 124
    licensing of 2, 16–7, 20–33, 57, 95, 98–101, 103, 120–2
    living and working conditions xix, 2–8, 10–3, 20–1, 36, 47–8, 50–3, 55–7, 60, 80–2, 91–4, 97, 102, 116–8, 124–6
    public opinion of xix, xxi, 2–3, 9–13, 53, 79–82, 85, 87–97, 124, 126
    relations with government authorities xx, 2, 8–13, 16–33, 53–4, 56–60, 95–107, 109–10, 116–8, 123–6
    traffic violations 57, 90–2, 96–7, 102–4

Ujung Pandang 1–2, 5, 7, 11, 101
urbanisation 2, 12, 108, 112–4, 123

INDEX

Vehicle Registration Department
 (VRD) 29, 36–7, 60, 86, 95, 99–101, 103, 106

World War II 1, 12, 20, 47, 55, 58, 60, 80, 121, 124

Xiamen 30–1, 50

Yogjakarta 1, 3, 5–7, 10–1, 101